amy e. spiegel

Letting Go *of* Perfect

Women, Expectations, and Authenticity

PUBLISHING GROUP

NASHVILLE, TENNESSEE

Copyright © 2012 by Amy Spiegel
All rights reserved.
Printed in the United States of America

978-1-4336-7626-0

Published by B&H Publishing Group
Nashville, Tennessee

Amy Spiegel is represented by the literary agency of
Wolgemuth & Associates, Inc.

Dewey Decimal Classification: 248.843
Subject Heading: WOMEN \ CHRISTIAN LIFE \
SELF-REALIZATION

All Scripture is taken from the Holy Bible,
New International Version, copyright © 1973,
1978, 1984; used by permission.

. 2 3 4 5 6 7 8 9 • 16 15 14 13 12

Dedication

To Jim, my oasis in exile, my best editor and loudest cheerleader; and to Bailey, Sam, Maggie, and Andrew who ate more pancake dinners than were good for them in order that my dream might come true.

Contents

FOREWORD

We've heard the story.

Woman meets man. Woman falls in love. Woman gets married. Woman has babies. Women wants to love Jesus fully, but she just can't seem to manage all of it at once and the bottom falls out a little bit. She doesn't love what she sees in the mirror every morning, and she certainly doesn't fall asleep feeling like she has accomplished all of her "this will make the day complete" lists.

The truth is, I was never very fazed when friends of mine got married and had kids, because I was certain that they just weren't good time-managers. I am efficient to the core. I can wash dishes, scrub counters, read storybooks, answer phone calls, and change diapers as I cook dinner. It can't be all that hard to do what I need to do to keep things going, right?

The truth is, if you had met me when my first two were babies, you might have believed me. I kept things orderly. I was Suzie-homemaker with two little red-headed cuties, and I always had make-up on. I don't know why I am still impressed by this, but I am. Nice work, Ang.

But under the make-up? Different story.

I was still pretty early in my marriage, and I underestimated what a good marriage needed in order to thrive. I was relatively young in my faith as well, and, you guessed it . . . I wasn't spending the kind of time I should have with the Lord.

I was exhausted. I was disappointed in myself. I was trying too hard to be something God never created me to be.

I know its nearly impossible in this life of "I'm just trying to get to the cash register without seeing twenty magazines that make me feel ugly," but we have to surround ourselves with people who speak truth to our ragged souls.

Amy Spiegel is one of those people, and I treasured reading her words because they reminded me that behind every woman we encounter is a story that can't be told from her lipstick or her minivan. What I love about Amy is that she can artfully manage to talk about free-range organic meat, homeschooling, and Target in a ten-page span. I need women like this in my world, who understand where I'm coming from when I say I'm tired of working so hard to still be such a mess.

There have been many, many days since my youngest were babies that I still feel like I'm falling off the treadmill in many ways. I wake up time and time again with a mile-long set of expectations and I usually fail by breakfast. It's in our nature to chase after the world, whether it's in the grocery store or in the bathroom mirror. But we have a living God who woos us in all of those places if we will only listen. Our identity is there, with Him, and I daily commit myself to believing that truth above all the other noise.

I'm so grateful for one more woman stepping up to the plate and sharing her heart so that we can see more of His. Well, done, Amy. I hope to hug your neck in a Target one day and thank you in person.

So, to all of you "imperfect" women—welcome to the club.

Make yourself at home, and don't mind the dishes in the sink . . . I'm trying to get my priorities in order and they didn't make it on to the list today. :)

Angie Smith
Author
What Women Fear and *I Will Carry You*

Introduction

One night, during that short stage of life between coming out from under my parents' wings and starting a nest of my own, I went out dancing with friends. A friend was to meet us there and amidst the sea of twenty-somethings, he missed our table. So I hopped up to chase after him only to have my way blocked by another twenty-something. I stepped to the side as did she, in that awkward side-stepping dance we sometimes perform. I looked up to laugh at our mutual error and thought to myself, *Isn't she cute,* a split second before I realized that "she" was in fact me.

I was facing a mirror and side-stepping with my own reflection. Awkward.

Fast-forward a decade or so and add a minivan full of kids. I am no longer a twenty-something, and my nights out are more likely to be spent be-bopping down the grocery aisle or vegging out watching the latest chick flick, an exhausted ball of sweatpants and fuzzy socks. I'm not complaining.

Okay, maybe just a little, but this is my life as a wife and mom, and for the most part I am content. But there are times when I feel as though I am back in that club, thumping dance music replaced by the thumping of my dryer, the hum of conversation replaced by squeals of mischievous delight from the bathtub. I'm standing at the mirror, studying an unrecognizable "me." I certainly don't long to go back but neither do I desire to be pulled along by the currents.

Attempting to maintain my own sense of self often feels like a nearly impossible balancing act in the midst of this life, so much of which is dedicated to the needs of others. So many of the women I know seem to feel the same tension in their own lives, tottering on the edge, praying someone will be there to catch them if they fall. They might not be faced with the same responsibilities that I have. Some are single with jobs that demand a great deal of energy and outside commitments that consume the rest. Some are older and facing the phase of life that brings the additional responsibilities of grandchildren and aging parents.

I recently attended a prayer group of godly, sincere women, each of whom I admire and respect. I had come to the group disheartened about my own shortcomings and, frankly, feeling a bit intimidated by the "accomplishments" of the rest of the group. These were the cover girls for Christian womanhood. Smart, "together," the kind of ladies that you suspect of wearing capes and leggings underneath their clothes, ready to dash into a nearby phone booth in case of an emergency. I sat in my chair dreading my time to share. I was there to share my prayer requests and lighten my load of worries and concerns, but all I wanted to do was hide under the coffee table and hope no one noticed me. I was faced with two choices—either be real and share about how ashamed I was of all the ways I had fallen short in the last few weeks . . . or lie. As I sat deflated, contemplating my rock and my hard place, the atmosphere began to change. Gone were the superheroes of my imagination. As the evening went on, and the cookies and hot tea worked their magic, woman after woman opened up about her insecurities, fears, and weaknesses. I didn't know whether to rejoice in the fact that I wasn't the only one struggling to keep my head above water or weep at the burden we each seemed to be laboring under.

When I left my beloved mountains in Tennessee and took up residence with my new husband amidst the cornfields of Indiana, I must confess to feeling ill at ease in the Midwest. I had attended Taylor University, the college where my husband Jim was and still is a philosophy professor, so Upland, Indiana, wasn't new to me, but it wasn't home. Permanently settling in Indiana, however, wasn't exactly what I had envisioned my future life to be. Giving up the rolling hills of my birthplace for the flat plains of my new home wasn't easy, but this was nothing compared to the journey I was soon to undertake.

Having only recently returned to an obedient pursuit of my faith, I was eager to be not only a good wife (and not long after, mother) but also a faithful servant in the church and to those around me. In my passion to pursue the Christian life to my utmost, I was on a perilous journey that could easily have ended in disaster when my situation failed to live up to my daydream version of the world or when my ability to meet life's challenges fell short of my lofty goals. The dangers of this journey had little to do with any major obstacles in my circumstances, though a fear of frostbite and hypothermia often prevent my leaving the house in the dead of winter. No, the perils I faced were those of my own making—the heavy burden of expectations I carried along the way. In my pursuit of perfection, I was nearly crushed beneath the weight of my idealized version of reality.

"It was the best of times, it was the worst of times" might have been a good description of the French Revolution by Charles Dickens, but it is also a very apt summation of the period of life in which I currently find myself. My life is one of contradictions. I long to serve God and show gratitude for my deliverance, but that service often feels more like a burdensome load than an offering of thanksgiving. I have volunteered for the job of wife and mother, and yet sometimes I feel more like a draftee than a volunteer. Despite my longing for close and meaningful friendships with other women, all too often I walk away from a girls' night out or weekly Bible study feeling defeated rather than refreshed. Being a parent brings great joy, but there are days when I am quite certain I have lost the ability to laugh. Kept on my toes more than a UN peacekeeper in a war zone and yet fighting boredom as I feel parts of my brain beginning to atrophy, I face constant noise and motion as well as deep isolation. My life: one minute I love it and know I am right where God wants me; the next minute I loathe it and feel that I have been misplaced and forgotten.

Now I have seen plenty of depictions of the modern woman: urban singles focused on their career and landing a man, suburban moms chauffeuring their well-groomed children from one mind-enriching event to another, harried moms struggling to keep it together by a thread, perfect wives with perfect hair and makeup, cleaning their perfect house and toning their perfect behinds—but none of those reflect the seeming paradoxes of my experience. As I said, we live in a college town in the heart of the heartland. In many ways this is an ideal setting for not only settling down and raising a family but for encountering a great cross section of women. My friends run the gamut from young college women still trying to figure out what they want to be when they grow up to retired women enjoying their grandkids. Ours is a community of thoughtful, committed Christian friends and families. Our kids have a slew of good friends as well as all the opportunities the university provides for their enrichment. (Who needs Carnegie Hall and Broadway when you have the university Jazz Band and *The Taming of the Shrew* on stage?) This community is often referred to as the "Taylor Bubble," but I suspect variations of this bubble have existed ever since the Puritans landed at Plymouth Rock and still exist wherever a Christian community is to be found.

In no way do I want to disparage the community that has brought me this far, supporting and encouraging me in countless ways. However, there is a downside to everything, and living in an evangelical community, academic or otherwise, is no exception. The temptation to compare and compete is constantly lurking in the shadows of every social event, waiting to bite you in the behind and leave your ego bruised. As Christian women, have we set the bar too high for ourselves? Are we striving to achieve our own version of the American dream—some sort of "Focus on the Family" all-star clan where the kids all love each other, while also reading above grade level and excelling in at least two extracurricular activities?

The night I left that prayer meeting, full of super-women who were willing to share their weaknesses and struggles, marked the beginning of a spiritual journey. I was going out in search of the freedom I had been promised. In search of the joy and peace I knew I was missing. Along the way, I would lay down my burdens of guilt and feelings of inadequacy only to double back, pick them up again, and repeat the process. I was on my way to letting go of perfect.

In this book I hope to burst the Christian bubble a bit or at least expose some of the myths that surround it. Not the Christian bubbles of truth and grace. Those things are not bubbles at all; those are the unchanging building blocks of our faith. The bubble I'm aiming at is that man-made construction of expectations and stereotypes that steal our joy and make us crazy. Bursting that bubble means discovering the truth about how the gospel, the good news, brings meaning to our everyday lives.

The good news of the gospel is brought by nail-scarred feet. It is that we have been given a new identity in Christ. It's as if we are turning state's evidence against our former crime family and have been put into the witness protection program. Only this new identity isn't based on false documents and fabricated background stories. We aren't just pretending to be someone else, someone new. We *are* someone new. So how does this reality inform the way we live our lives? How does it change the way we see our callings, our relationships, our suffering and blessings? As we strive to serve with excellence in our new family, how do we remain authentic to the terms of our adoption? These are some of the questions I set out to wrestle with in writing this book.

I am no family expert. My kids are the ones running amuck after church with Kool-Aid stained shirts and permanent grass stains on their jeans. I am no Martha Stewart. I don't know how to fold napkins properly and make breakfast for dinner at least twice a week. I am just a woman, trying to get it right, holding tight to Jesus, and seeking His grace in the little things as well as the big. In sharing my journey, which is still very much in process, I hope to encourage you in yours.

Speaking at our church's annual women's conference, I was introduced by a friend who started with my basic background, where I went to college, number of kids, etc. She ended by saying something that touched me deeply and perfectly summed up the reasons I had for wanting to write this book. She said that after talking with me, she always felt like I was on her side. In writing this book, I hope to give you that same feeling. Not that there is someone far in the distance, calling on you to catch up but someone who is walking alongside just like you. Someone who is cheering you on. Someone who is on your side. It is my wish that, together, we can let go of our own expectations, let go of our version of perfection, in order to find the perfection of Christ.

Chapter One

A Series of Fortunate Events

*If you are interested in stories with happy endings, you
would be better off reading some other book.*
—Lemony Snicket, *A Series of Unfortunate Events*

The clock is ticking. The baby is crying. The toddler
is tearing the house apart. I have exactly minus-two
minutes before I am officially really, really late. All the
still-warm cookies for my husband's class are neatly stacked
in a decorative basket, waiting to be delivered with a smile
and a "Don't mention it" from "the wife." All I have to do
is throw my breakfast shake in the blender and run—I do
mean run—out the door, pulling the kids with me by the
sheer force of my desperation.

And then it happens.

The makeshift blender top (a paper towel hastily snatched when the real one was nowhere to be found) drops into the swirling milk and Slim Fast and a torrent of milky brownness sprays across my clothes and all over the floor. I look down at the only semi-hip outfit that fits me anymore and burst into tears. I fall to my knees, torn between cleaning up the mess and the lateness of the hour. I alternate between hysterical laughter and rage.

The clock is ticking. The baby is crying. The toddler is running for cover. And I wonder, how on earth did I get to this place?

I am an avid reader and film buff and have a special place in my heart for the Victorians. Though she predates the Victorian period, I hold Jane Austen in the highest regard and am quite confident she will be my best friend in heaven. After a long day slogging through laundry and emptying the dishwasher *again*, I love nothing better than cuddling up for a little trip to Pemberly or a cup of tea with my dear friend *Emma*. Of course, in novels they never show the heroine burning dinner or yelling at the kids to go to sleep. Maybe that's why I like Austen so much.

If the story of my husband Jim and I was a novel, one would never guess the ending from our rather inauspicious start. The first time I met my husband Jim, I was a freshman at Taylor University and Jim was starting his first year as a professor in Taylor's philosophy department. It was my job to interview him for an article to be featured in Taylor's yearbook and, to be honest, I found him to be a bit abstract and seemingly condescending. Little did I know that at the time he was in the midst of a trying and difficult time of personal upheaval. While most college students might be too mature to believe in the myth that teachers have no life outside of the classroom, they sometimes behave as if this were the case. I walked away from our first encounter with something more akin to annoyance than butterflies in my stomach. Silly girl.

Over my three years at Taylor, we got to know one another through mutual friends and while there were no romantic sparks, I greatly enjoyed talking with Jim. I had never met someone who was so morally serious and yet so interesting to me. (Jim's perception of these "pop-in" appearances at his office was a bit different. I think he would, at the time at least, have considered it more like a recurring haunting presence rather than neighborly visits.) In college I considered myself interesting but definitely not morally serious. I had chosen Taylor—a conservative Christian college—through some ironic plan of providence. Despite the fact that I am from a great family of faith, I had not made that faith my own. It was for the best that Jim's being a professor and my being a student created a natural barrier for any relationship beyond friendship since at the time I was wrapped up in a bohemian package with long hair, baggy clothes, and a pack-a-day smoking habit. You begin to see why Jim wasn't chomping at the bit to take me out for dinner and a movie.

After graduating and moving back to my hometown of Knoxville, Tennessee, I realized the folly of my ways and while I still had a long way to go (and still do for that matter), I was on the road to reformation. A series of fortunate events threw Jim and me together again and—finding that I was now both morally serious and interesting (not to mention very interested in him)—Jim agreed to give dating a chance. Less than a year later, we were married, much to the delight of friends and family.

Jim and I were married in March of 1998 in the beautiful little town of Norris, Tennessee. My sister Susan says I marched down the aisle like a stallion out of the gate, and while I don't feel exactly flattered by the comparison, I know the sentiment is true. Our wedding day was the happiest day of my life. But little did I know that in walking down the aisle (I know I didn't trot or gallop), my journey was just beginning.

In the months before we started dating, I had begun to wrestle with what I really believed and how those beliefs needed to be reflected in my choices. Now as a wife, I would have to wrestle with how my identity as a child of God impacted my most intimate relationship, that with my husband. Just as the truth regarding grace and what it means to be forgiven had begun to soak in for me as an individual, I would now have to wrestle with the same ideas as I took on the role of a wife.

One of my first wrestling matches was with the truth

regarding the consequences of our choices. It's funny how when you say "yes" to something (like the man of your dreams), you don't think about the fact that you are also saying "no" to something else. If you order a cheeseburger, you don't really stop to think about the fact that what you are in fact doing is saying no to everything else on the menu (except for maybe some fries and milk shake, but you get the point). Part of growing up is narrowing your life choices to a manageable size. I rarely envy my husband's students with all their "What will I do with my life?!" anxiety, but there are times when I turn a slightly greenish shade at all of the possibilities that lie before them.

When I accepted the honor of Jim's affection, I made a decision to reject all other possible futures. Though there has never come a time when I wished for another husband, he came with a set of circumstances that I hadn't necessarily thought through. Jim is a college professor in rural (and I mean *rural*) Indiana. It is a far cry, not to mention a long car ride, from my beloved East Tennessee, as well as most of my family. I may have marched down that aisle ready to go, but there would be times down the road where my resolve would be tested, not by any great temptation but rather by the seductive lulling to sleep that is familiarity.

As you settle in for the long ride, sometimes you can forget just how spectacular your traveling companion is. You start to stare out the window at the passing landscape and begin to wonder if you really are headed in the right direction. That is when it is essential to have fixed landmarks along the way to remind you why you started the journey to begin with. So on the days when I long for the rolling hills of my homeland or Jim doesn't have time to chat on the phone while I try to keep the barbarians (aka our kids) at bay, I can look back in my mind's eye to those days of fevered love not with a sigh of nostalgia but with confidence that I am going in the right direction. This doesn't always fill my heart with deep joy and affection, but it keeps me on course. And on those days when I must choose between five more minutes of sleep and a quick perusal of a passage in the Bible, I can think back on the sunny Sunday when I sat in my apartment and cried out to God, telling Him I was miserable trying to run things on my own anymore. Giving over control to Him means acting in obedience. Submitting my will to His may not always be easy but remembering the misery of doing things *my* way certainly makes it easier.

That doesn't mean that I always pick up the Bible instead of snuggling in for a few more winks of sleep. But it does mean that I know where I have come from and I know where I am going.

Now that Jim and I are almost fifteen years into our less than likely fairy tale, I know why authors stop at happily-ever-after, because the truth is that there is no such thing, at least on this side of paradise. I never found the endings of *Cinderella* or *Snow White* particularly satisfying. Boy meets girl (in one case only sees her in a coma), and we are to believe that rosy lips and a pretty singing voice will see them through the next fifty years? I don't think so. However, the sunset of Elizabeth and Darcy's happily-ever-after (in *Pride and Prejudice*), with their deep affection and mutual respect proven over time, used to fill me with joy and evoke a sigh of great pleasure. As I have left my twenties behind and am barreling toward ages that round up to the big 4-0, I have noticed a longing for more. As I close the book on the last page or the credits start to roll, I find all the realities of married life clouding my once rose-tinted vision and begin to wonder, "Did they face financial setbacks? Does one of their children die? How do they settle their differences of opinion?"

Unfortunately for me, when I got married, I hadn't yet realized that in the real world the wedding isn't the ending credits. Like those Pixar shorts before the feature presentation, your wedding day is great but has little to do with your actual married life. It wasn't as if I thought Jim and I would never argue or face difficulties. I just hadn't really thought much about it. I knew this was the man I was supposed to marry and was content to go about the business of doing so while leaving the rest (that is, the next several decades we would be spending together) for after the honeymoon.

As women, many of us have been given the gift of seeing the big picture; we are vision casters. This is a great gift to possess, however we can get so busy whipping our vision paint around with broad and nonspecific strokes that we forget to fill in all the details. While we have an image of the completed picture in our mind's eye, the details of how to achieve the end product are a little fuzzy. We have the vision without necessarily the skills and patience to bring it to fruition and it's sometimes a surprise that it is far more difficult to complete the picture than to conceive it.

When Jim and I began to settle in together, it was a jolt. Of course, I had had close quarters relationships before with my family and roommates but never as a sincere believer. I assumed any discord in the past was due to my disobedient lifestyle and that now that I was more devout, everything would be smooth sailing. I filled a great deal of my time picking fights with my husband over the most meaningless topics possible trying to get to the source of my irritation, not realizing that I and my sinful heart were the source.

The odd result of my seemingly constant need to pick fights with my husband wasn't a diminishing of my love and affection for him, but rather a deep conviction of my own sin. I knew Jim, despite the average number of faults we all have, was a great guy. I was crazy about him. So if it wasn't his fault, then it must be mine. What kind of person drives her spouse to despair over such trivial matters? Apparently, the kind of person *I* was, and I found this idea disconcerting to say the least. I didn't want to talk to people or go out because I hated feeling like a fraud. I felt that by making small talk and chatting with people I was deceiving them into believing that I was a nice person. I began to see that sin was not just an instance of moral failure on my part like a mole or tumor you can have removed. Instead, *I* was a mole or tumor. The cancer of sin had spread through my entire body and penetrated every aspect of my soul.

I don't know if I had ever heard of the idea of total depravity, the view that every aspect of our nature has been corrupted by sin and that without God's intervention we can do nothing to save ourselves. Either I wasn't paying attention that day in Sunday school or it wasn't emphasized in the church I grew up attending. Having been a rebellious teenager and young adult, I just assumed that it was my rebelliousness that caused my sinful behavior. But I wasn't living in rebellion anymore and so I initially (and naively) assumed that the weakness that did "the evil I do not want to do" (Rom. 7:19) would slowly fade away and I would behave like the person I wanted to be. When this didn't happen, I had to come to grips with the fact that I was saved, yes, but not yet fully transformed. While this time was demoralizing, it was necessary. If I wanted to move forward, not only in my relationship with Jim but also with God, I had to get some things straight first. The most important of these was that I was not a nice person. I could be nice on occasion but my nature was one of corruption and sin. And this isn't just true of myself but of all mankind. When David says in Psalm 51 "Surely I was sinful at birth, sinful from the time my mother conceived me," he wasn't just referring to himself but all of us. This is a very bleak diagnosis for the human race but when the truth of this fact really pierced my heart it was like lancing a boil. I wasn't any less sick or any less deficient but my sickness had a name, and I wasn't alone in my suffering. And I would discover, though in reality I already knew this truth in my head, I wasn't without cure.

To be honest, I can't remember how the fog began to lift. I am sure it was through a series of smaller revelations—teetering, wobbly baby steps toward the truth. In the slower-paced, lazy atmosphere of summer, tensions eased and I began to make peace with the truth of my nature. I started to think maybe I wasn't such a monster after all. The truth didn't end with my sinfulness but the work of Jesus on my behalf. Of course, I completely affirmed His death for my sins. I needn't fear God's wrath or judgment, but He still had work to do and marriage was a big part of that work. I had assumed that the selfishness and pride that was bubbling to the surface of my heart was a sign that something was wrong. In fact, something was wrong, but not what I thought. I thought that because Jim and I did things to annoy one another that this meant there was something wrong with our relationship. Actually there really wasn't anything wrong with our marriage other than the fact that we were both fallen human beings. God ordained marriage not as a source of endless enjoyment and pleasure but as a means of sanctification. We are being refined by one another and the process isn't pretty, but it *is* productive.

When I realized that Jim was being used as a tool for my betterment and I for him, a weight was lifted. I am not his wife to provide for his happiness, though thankfully for us happiness was a bonus. I am his wife to give him opportunities to be gracious, forgiving, and kind. He isn't my husband to make me feel loved and special all the time, though he often does. He is my husband to give me opportunities to see myself as I really am and in humility strive to change. In marriage, and later in parenting, we are able to display characteristics (good and bad) that would otherwise be unknown to us and have an opportunity for them to shine (the good) and to change (the bad).

My sister once wisely told me that God chooses our spouse with all of our weaknesses in mind. She reasoned that perhaps our husbands are exactly calculated by Him to irritate us in all the ways that we need irritating and the same is true for us. While not exactly a picture of roses and romance or something explicitly taught in Scripture, my sister's insight is very liberating. In this light my failings aren't wasted but can actually be of use. I shouldn't jump on Jim's flaws in an attempt to change *him*. Instead, I can see them as occasions for grace on my part and times of reflection on what my annoyance reveals about my own heart.

Once I grasped this concept, everything seemed less urgent and dire. And in the days to come, as we went from a couple to a family, I would need to remind myself of this over and over again. I am not here to make my children happy in a fleeting, earthly way, though I try my hardest. We are all surrounded by people who annoy us and are annoyed by us in turn. Rather than seeing them as obstacles to be removed or reshaped, we must embrace them as instruments of grace being used for our own betterment. Our identity as God's children isn't one of perfection, but a picture of His grace. This perspective, along with a firm grasp of our own sinful nature, should humble us in the face of relational difficulties but also encourage us in the face of adversity.

The clock has ceased its ticking. The baby is laughing in his daddy's arms while being paraded around the class for all to see and admire. The chocolate-faced toddler is happily drawing formless blobs on the dry erase board. The cookies have been safely delivered into the hands of Jim's students, and my outfit, while not so hip or flattering is without food smudges (for the time being anyway). As the students file out of class, smiling at the kids, many stop to say thanks, to which I reply, "Don't mention it." Maybe there are a few happy endings this side of heaven after all. We just aren't the ones who get to write them.

Chapter Two

Vanity's Flair

A woman may possess the wisdom and chastity
of Minerva, and we give no heed to her,
if she has a plain face. What folly will not a pair
of bright eyes make pardonable? What dullness
may not red lips and sweet accents render pleasant?
—William Makepeace Thackeray (*Vanity Fair*)

Sitting in the parking lot of our local Arby's, I feel the stir again—the ever-present mixture of kicking feet and rumbling tummy, both pleading to be fed. *Now, baby (and stomach), I just sacrificed four cheesy and delicious sticks of highly-processed dairy on the altar of your hunger. Surely you are satisfied and we can head home for a much-needed nap.* The rumbling and kicking only increase—a decided "No" from the nether regions of my abdomen. Sighing, I put the car into gear. *All right, if you insist.*

Heading for the drive-thru window for the second time in the last ten minutes, I have no idea the price to be paid for my indulgences. But at the moment I am on a sort of layaway program. Nine months of totally extravagant excess to be paid (with interest) farther down the road.

For most of us our childhood and teen years are mostly spent assuming that just as the planets revolve around the sun, the world revolves around us. In our adult lives, however, we take baby steps in a journey toward a deeper understanding of our own selfishness and sin. We get roommates and coworkers, fellow committee members and spouses, and suddenly a metaphorical lightbulb illuminates our minds and we start to understand that the world is not in fact me-centric. This can be painful but it's part of the process of growing up. For me and, I suspect, many other women, married life was a mirror in which I saw the reflection of my inner selfishness and sin. Pregnancy and its aftermath, however, was a giant billboard on the highway of life displaying my vanity and pride.

Of course, you don't have to be a mother-in-waiting to realize the depth of your superficiality. (Is it possible for superficiality to have depth?) We are submerged in a culture where entire magazines are dedicated to the sculpting of our rear ends and the ripping of our abs. Victoria's Secret "fashion shows" are treated like sporting events, and one sees more cleavage walking down the grocery store aisle than at a Hugh Hefner pool party. The struggle to keep our heads above water and avoid drowning in a sea of either self-loathing or self-worship is constant. We are faced with the temptation to constantly rank ourselves, and everyone around us, on the scale of fitness or, if we are honest, the scale of thinness. Going to the gym or the neighborhood pool may be a challenge for men to keep their thoughts pure and lust-free. But I would venture to guess that just as many women struggle to keep their thoughts free of envy and pride.

This struggle is a universal one for women, but how should we, as Christian women overcome it? What gospel-centered principles can we exercise that can help shape our values and thoughts like so many leg lifts shape our inner thighs? How do we avoid the extremes of legalism and immodesty? The experience of pregnancy not only brings many of these issues to light for those who have experienced it personally but also serves as a great metaphor for women exploring the question of vanity and all its fallout.

I certainly struggled with body image issues prepregnancy, but watching my body seemingly defy the laws of elasticity to the point of apparent impossibility, took all those insecurities and pride and highlighted them . . . in really bright colors . . . with bold print and underlining for emphasis. Pride is an easy sin to live with when you don't have a stomach the size of a watermelon. During my pregnancies, I watched my once relatively toned skin expand and contract over and over, like a balloon that has been inflated beyond its recommended capacity. As the outward signs of each child's impending birth grew, the inward realities of my prideful heart grew as well. I might not have been able to see my own feet, but my vanity was clearly showing.

In the same way that children start out as a single cell, hidden deep within our bodies, growing and taking root, sin often starts out as a small thought, which left to itself will grow larger over time. Harboring these little zygotes of disobedience seems harmless enough at the time but—left to their own devices—they will continue to grow. This is true of all sin, but I think there is a soft spot in the hearts of the daughters of Eve for vanity and her best friend pride.

Within the confines of our sin-infected hearts, these seeds of mutinous discontentment are not only created but find fertile soil in which to grow and flourish. They are not foreign invaders. The manure of overexposure to the parades of artificially breast-inflated anorexics which stream through our televisions, movie theaters, and checkout aisles certainly helps bend our hearts and minds in the wrong directions. However, vanity and all her siblings are our own offspring, born and bred inside our own skin; they are the enemy from within. Though our spirits, made alive in Christ, may wish to repel them, our flesh, born in Eve's first teeth-sinking bite, embraces them as their own.

I suffer from selective amnesia when it comes to my children's babyhoods (perhaps the months—slipping into years—of sleep deprivation have something to do with that), but I do remember with great clarity the moment my husband and I learned that each of them was on the way. There is something magical, not to mention a little frightening, about discovering that you are pregnant, even if it isn't your first time around the gestational merry-go-round. A little secret that, for a moment or two, only you (and the little stick you just peed on) know. There is something sacred in the secret. You and this little being will share your body for the next forty weeks in the most intimate of relationships, and—for now—only you (and the pee stick) know it.

Obviously, however, it doesn't stay this way. Whether you take out a full-page ad or keep it on the down-low, eventually the truth becomes self-evident. You are pregnant, with child, in the family way.

People, some of whom you hardly know, will begin to comment on your belly size. They might even give it a rub, like you have strapped an animal of some kind to your front side and given total strangers permission to pet you at their leisure. It is as if, despite the fact that you are quite obviously attached to your midsection, that area of your body has suddenly been zoned for public use (as well as public discourse). This is one of the aspects of pregnancy for which

I was entirely unprepared. I never realized just what a communal affair having a baby could be or how uncomfortable the communal aspect of reproducing would make me feel. I am not one who enjoys having my physical appearance commented on. I am horribly self-conscious at the best of times, let alone when I am roughly the size of a beluga whale. So when Joe Churchgoer and Susie Grocery-Cashier started asking about how far along I was or noting my belly size, I did not take kindly to it.

It seems a bit cruel that people choose to comment on the size and shape of a woman's body during pregnancy, the time when most women would happily become invisible. Why is it that OB/GYNs choose to place their scales in the front of the office? Have mercy, for pity's sake. There is no more dreaded sound for an expecting mother than the sound of that medal bar sliding into place at the top of the scale, signifying the growing distance between your waistline and your prepregnancy jeans.

Because of the public nature of pregnancy, women lose a certain degree of autonomy in the process of becoming mothers. We become a part of something ancient and communal. Ancient in that despite the years that separate us from all that have come before us, the process, plus or minus better maternity clothes and pain management drugs, has remained basically the same. And communal in that millions of women over thousands of years have conceived, carried, and given birth, from the moment of conception until that final push.

We are not only connected to the community of women

over the span of time but also to this new life. No longer only an individual, we are connected in the most profound of ways to another human being. This is, in many ways, a great privilege. You know, the whole Hand-That-Rocks-The-Cradle-Rules-The-World thing.

I am not terribly crafty, but a few years back I learned how to make friendship bracelets for the kids and their friends. Never had I known the sense of crafty accomplishment I felt when tying on those bracelets. It's sad, I know, but we can't all be Martha Stewart. How much more pride, in the healthy sense of the term, should I feel for having knit together four human beings! And yet the mystical union of mother and child isn't without its drawbacks. You are physically connected to another human being. It takes Ruth's sentiments of "Where you go, I will go" to a whole new level. "What you eat, I will eat. When you grow, I will grow. My heart beat is your life's blood." While not all of us have the experience of pregnancy, as believers in Christ we have a similar experience of becoming part of a body. That is, we function as elements within a great whole. When we make that leap of faith into the body of Christ, we too lose a great deal of our autonomy, as we now serve a cause greater than our own personal desires and whims.

Again, this enmeshing of flesh has its pros and cons. Suddenly we are supported all around by those who have the same overall goals and beliefs that we have. Sure, we have individual callings and perspectives on the best way to achieve them, but we have Jesus as our head (Eph. 4:15), guiding and directing us. We have the Holy Spirit working within our own hearts but also communing with our fellow saints and creating unity of mind and spirit. You might have guessed those, and many others, are the pros. I suppose the cons aren't truly cons at all, depending on your perspective. They are cons to our fleshly nature that squirms and wiggles, desperate to break free from all accountability and restraint. The cons of the body are the pros of the spirit. What the body sees as restrictive boundaries, the spirit sees as protective unity.

If we are connected, then what I do directly affects you. It's not just that if I am rude it hurts your feelings, but that what I do impacts the overall health of the body. A few too many slices of pizza doesn't just give my stomach a hard time but reeks havoc on my whole digestive system or a sinus infection doesn't just make my face hurt but drains energy from everywhere else in my body. My selfish behavior doesn't just slow *my* sanctification process; it inhibits my church's ability to minister to those in our community. It sets a bad example for my children that they are likely to follow rather than reject. It prevents my husband from fulfilling his vocation to the utmost because he is busy carrying more than his fair share of household chores or listening to me whine regarding trivial matters.

As a professor's wife, I have many opportunities to observe college-aged women living in community and, while bootcut may be replaced with skinny, there are discussions and struggles that remain constant. One of those regards modesty. Often the discussion seems to focus on the responsibility women have to consider the struggles of men. While I certainly think this is an appropriate part of the discussion, I wonder if it is also appropriate to consider what responsibility we as women have to one another and ourselves. While I now have been around the birthing floor a time or four, am over thirty and love cheese too much to be letting anything above the knee hang out, this wasn't always the case. I am sorry to say that my foray into modest dress was more of a forced retreat rather than a voluntary march. However I got there, my time in the modesty trenches has taught me that choosing what I will and won't wear is as much about living up to my responsibilities to myself and my fellow womankind as it is showing consideration to my brothers.

I have a responsibility not to create a competitive or hostile environment for my fellow females. By dressing more conservatively, we lessen the temptation to envy and compare, allowing the spirit to overrule the flesh, so to speak. I have noticed for myself that both my inner and outward dialogue tend to be more edifying while chatting in baggy sweats rather than in my "skinny" jeans. (For me, this referred not to a style of jeans but rather "Jeans I have to lay down on the bed in order to zip.") Of course, it is my responsibility to not allow my mind to wander into the land of unhealthy thoughts just because Suzie SkinnyBum looks better in spandex than I do. But in a culture that encourages women to maintain weights at which they are actually digesting their brains for lack of nourishment, surely we can help a girl out and wear pants that don't require surgical removal. Maybe you look great in them, but that isn't really the point. In fact, your choice in outerwear isn't the point at all.

Maybe you would never wear curve-clinging denim, but you go to great lengths to present your children to the world perfectly groomed and color coordinated. Or maybe you fret over unplucked eyebrows or that belly fat that refuses to disappear. Whatever the focus of your vanity, there is nothing wrong with looking nice, but we need to consider our motives and the impact our actions have. Just as a mother-to-be swallows those nasty prenatal vitamins each morning or chooses the glass of water over the caffeine-laden soda, we are called to swallow our pride and vanity for the good of the body or push away our freedom in order that others might not stumble.

It isn't only for the sake of others, however, that I plug my nose and take my medicine like a good girl. I have recently made two changes in my life that have greatly increased my ability to feel comfortable in my own skin and that comfort, I hope, is beneficial to the whole team. About a year and a half ago, my friend Carrie gently challenged me to consider running. Not running out the door to escape my children or running to the freezer for another ice cream bar but running for the sake of exercise. This challenge has started me on a journey to take my health more seriously. A few times a week, another friend, Kristin, and I get together, sweat like pigs, and spur one another on toward fitness. This is, of course, another potential beachhead for competitiveness, but instead it has been an opportunity for community. I feel as if we are in this together, and I love seeing her eke out two more push-ups when I am lying defeated in a pool of sweat. In a way it feels as though her accomplishments are mine. And while the treadmill may seem the perfect breeding ground for conceit, I haven't found that to be the case. Because it isn't about what I am doing in the aerobics room, it's about what is going on inside my head.

As I have become proud of my own accomplishments, I have found it easier to be proud of others. Maybe working out isn't your thing, but we should all have areas of our lives where we celebrate our own abilities. Not in order to put others down, but rather to lift up the body as a whole.

The other part of this journey has been putting a great deal more thought into the clothes I choose. This may seem like a contradiction, trying to become *less* vain by thinking *more* about the way I look. But it is the direction of those thoughts not the quantity that really counts. Now when I get dressed, rather than thinking about whether or not this outfit makes my rear end look big, I try to concentrate on whether or not this outfit makes my values look small. I have gotten great pleasure in really taking stock of my wardrobe and getting rid of those things that don't really reflect my inner landscape. Of course, this has also given me an excuse for going out and buying new clothes in the name of spiritual development. Every woman should think about how the way she dresses impacts her own spirit as well as that of those around her. There is no Christian woman uniform, but there are definitely principles we can all consider when we head for our closets each morning *and* when we judge the choices others have made.

My daughter has inherited her mother's legendary opinionated nature when it comes to fashion. She can rock a striped dress with plaid leggings like a runway model. When heading out the door, I often walk a fine line between allowing for self-expression and enabling a fashion disaster. When it comes to modesty, I try to keep a high standard; when it comes to color coordination, not so much. I hope my sisters in Christ will show me the same grace, gently calling me on the carpet if I wander into the inappropriate while biting their tongues at the just-not-my-style.

The clothes you wear speak for your values and beliefs. We all must take care that they whisper our love of each other rather than screaming out our vanity. If we are nurturing the life inside of each of us, the life of the spirit, it will show on the outside. Just as the expanding belly of a woman in the family way tells of the life she is carrying, our new inner life will be made evident in our outward choices. If maternity tops and elastic waist jeans are the signs that say "Baby on Board," how can we clad ourselves in such a way that says "Vanity in Check"? The next time you are heading out the door, pause at the mirror and make sure that what you see reflects your purpose and values. That doesn't mean donning the burka, but it probably doesn't mean having words on your butt either.

Staring in the mirror, I feel the stir again; the ever-present mixture of pride and loathing, pleading to be fed. *Now, flesh-child, I have sacrificed too many thoughts to you already. Surely you are satisfied and we can rest now.* My fleshly eyes are tempted to dwell on the stretch marks and cellulite bubbles and call them shame. I pray for my spiritual eyes to be opened to these battle scars, these marks of life lived and given and call them joy. I will not indulge the creature within, not today at least. Pulling on my clothes, I walk away knowing that I am on a sort of layaway plan; purchased, not with gold or silver but with blood. I am just waiting to be picked up and taken home. Until then, I will wait and do my best to make peace with the body in the mirror.

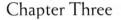

Chapter Three

Cries and Punishment

I did not bow down to you, I bowed down
to all the suffering of humanity.
—Fyodor Dostoevsky, *Crime and Punishment*

Screams cut through the night air, screams of sheer terror and despair. These are the desperate cries of a soul
searching for aid in the face of some mortal danger, crying
out into the darkness, hoping, praying to be rescued. But
no one comes and slowly the cries subside into resigned
whimpers, fading into heavy breathing. There comes a sigh
of surrender and then, silence.

It isn't that no one hears these cries. And it isn't that
those who hear don't care. In fact, they love the little soul

in question very much. And it is that love that keeps them frozen, longing to swoop in and comfort but knowing that after the crying and fighting, peace will come and the little soul will get what he needs. They are wiser than the little soul and though he may doubt their wisdom, they know that what seems, in his small mind, to be neglect or torture, is in reality love. For sometimes it is the things we don't do that show how much we care. It is the silence that sings our love.

When my oldest son, Bailey, was a wee thing, still so fresh out of the oven you weren't quite sure he was done yet, we would snuggle him tight in his sweet-smelling pajamas and blanket and gently lay him down to sleep in his carefully color-coordinated room. We would tip-toe to the doorway, sneak one last look, and quietly shut the door. At which point, we would sit and listen to him scream for the next thirty minutes or so. From the volume of his pitiful cries, you would have thought we had just body slammed him into a den of vipers and walked away in complete indifference. We had read all the books about "teaching" your baby to sleep, though before becoming parents, the process seemed rather self-explanatory. After all we hadn't needed to teach him how to breathe, eat, or poop, and sleeping seemed to be right up there with the basic, instinctive functions of a human being. Nevertheless, we benefited from the authority of many childhood experts, cheering us on as we let our newborn son "cry it out."

There were plenty of times, however, we told the experts in our heads to take a hike and tried rocking Bailey into peaceful slumbers. Unfortunately it was less than effective and seemed only to upset him more. I suppose if you don't want to go to sleep, someone swaying you side to side and softly singing a random mix of Bob Dylan and lullabies in your ear would be rather annoying. This was, I am sure, a rather unpleasant way for our son to start his journey in this world, but for my husband and me, it was heartbreaking.

We are prepared as parents to *do* anything for our children. Jump in front of a bullet for them? Sure. Though one does struggle a bit to envision the scenario in which we would be called upon to do so, we would gladly take the hit. Walk barefoot over glass? No problem. We do this every day as we traverse a bedroom floor booby-trapped with innumerable jagged Lego pieces in order to bring one more cup of water or bestow one last good-night kiss. No, it often isn't what we are called upon to do for those we love but what we are required *not* to do that makes loving them so very hard.

Those nights Jim and I spent on the couch, huddled together for moral support, I felt my eyes being opened even as my son refused to close his. I began to understand not only the realities of earthly parenting but also how I am parented by my heavenly Father. Through those brief, but seemingly endless moments, I felt God the Father's bemused smile shining on me as I heard my own cries for rescue echoed in those of my child. How many nights had *I* lain in the darkness, both physical and spiritual, pleading to be rescued, doubting that anyone heard? How many nights had He been right outside my heart's door, waiting for all my flailing to cease? Waiting for me to be silent? Waiting for me to hear His love singing?

The experience of becoming a parent enlightened me a great deal on the subject of suffering and the role it plays in our lives. Parents serve as "god-like" entities in their children's lives, making the most of their decisions, demanding respect and obedience. Seeing things from this side of the discipline aisle has greatly changed my perception of God's dealings with me. This is especially true when it comes to situations I know He has ordained and yet I would rather not experience. How do we reconcile the knowledge that He loves and cares for us and yet allows us to experience pain and suffering?

Suffering is a funny thing—obviously not ha-ha funny, but funny in a strange way. Despite being surrounded by the suffering of others, despite news reports and prayer requests and forwarded e-mails that announce its presence in every corner of our acquaintance, somehow suffering always takes us by surprise.

My children *love* to try to frighten me. Walking through our home can often resemble trying to negotiate one's way through a bad haunted house at Halloween. Try as they might, they are as stealthy as elephants. Their small feet tread a bit too loudly or they can't resist peeping around the corner one more time to make sure I am headed in their direction. I generally feign surprise and give a half-hearted, "Oh, you really scared me. Now go make your bed." But the interesting thing is that, if I want to, I can always get them, even when they know it's coming. Because I am a cruel and insensitive mother, my favorite way of "getting them" is blowing the car horn just as they pass in front of the hood. Just a light tap, mind you, but it never fails to catch them off guard. Even when they make eye contact, just before the fatal blast, and even when they sense the maniacal twinkle in my eye, they always jump sky high, God bless 'em.

Why is that? Why is it that they are surprised by this sudden but entirely anticipatable interruption of their otherwise peaceful pathway to the car? I have done it countless times and yet they never see it coming while I, with the exception of some particularly cleverly conceived prank, rarely fail to anticipate their intent? My hunch is that it is a matter of perspective and experience, both of which children, through no fault of their own, are greatly lacking in. I know that whatever is going to jump out from around the corner can't hurt me while they still fear the unknown. I see it coming because I've been down that road before, while they are blindsided by something they have not yet learned to anticipate.

While I outshine my children in the category of "Least Likely to Be Startled," weathering the jump-out-and-get-ya moments of life is an entirely different beast, and one I fear I may never learn to tame. Despite the fact that these moments have been popping out from around corners all my life, I never seem to be prepared when they jump out

LETTING GO OF PERFECT

and say "Boo!" We all know that life is full of the unexpected and yet somehow it catches us off guard. This can
range from the mild annoyance of a flat tire or a poorly-
timed cold to the life-altering, I'm-so-scared-I-just-peed-in-
my-pants kind of moments such as a serious illness, broken
relationships, or death.

Ironically the first person to receive blame in the worst
of these cases is usually God. We turn to Him in angry
bewilderment and ask "Why?!" not just "Why has this
terrible thing happened to me?" but also "Why didn't
You warn me?" I say it's ironic because, of course, He has
warned us—repeatedly! The Bible is chock-full of warnings regarding the sufferings of this world, not to mention
that we are surrounded by everyday warnings, written into
the fabric of the natural world. You merely have to sit down
and watch the Discovery Channel to see the injustice of
a beautiful gazelle who is minding her own business one
minute and running for her life the next. Open the Bible
to read about Job, David, all of the prophets of the Old
Testament, and dozens more who suffered not only the
consequences of a fallen world but suffered more than
most because of their faithfulness to God. Psalms and
Proverbs are full of grim statements regarding the injus-
tices suffered by those who travel through this world, the
righteous and the unrighteous alike (see Ps. 44:23–25;
58:1–3; Hab. 1:1–3).

So why does it startle us? Why do we accept the blessings
of our lives as the status quo and suffering as the anomaly?
Not only that but the hardships seem to erase or negate all

the blessings with which we have been showered. I experience this phenomenon every time I take the kids somewhere fun. Upon entry to this little slice of heaven, whether it be the park or a trip to the Kiddie Casino (i.e., Chuck E. Cheese), I am immediately deemed the "Best Mom in the Whole World." I am showered with thank-yous, hugs, and kisses. Today is officially declared the "Best day ever!" If I am lucky and no one falls and scrapes a knee or gets cheated out of their tokens by a broken game, this euphoria will last for a few hours. However, as the moment of our departure nears, I brace myself for battle. For as soon as I say it's time to go (and mean it), I am immediately dethroned as Queen Mommy. Gone are the hugs and kisses of gratitude. They are supplanted by pouting lips, crossed arms, and other forms of sulky defiance. Gone are the shouts of joy and pleasure. Now there are only cries of lament and accusatory whining.

As much as I am annoyed by this behavior, aren't I often guilty of the same attitudes and assumptions, only perhaps more cleverly disguised? When God tells me it is time to leave the green pastures and head for the Valley of the Shadow of Death, don't I, too, stomp my foot and mutter under my breath? Just as my children's behavior reveals certain truths regarding their immature and selfish hearts, what does my ingratitude in the face of suffering reveal about my own attitudes and assumptions? In part, I assume that if God loves me, He will give me what I want. Not what He knows I need, or what is best for me, but what I desire. And if He withholds those things from me, then it doesn't mean that He is teaching me to want what is better.

Rather, it must mean that He doesn't care, or that I have done something to displease Him and therefore I am being punished. I may not affirm these things with my lips but in the secret places of my heart, I am on the floor, kicking and screaming, desperate to get my own way. I am Eve in the garden reaching for the forbidden fruit and sure that I know better than my Creator.

In the Garden we find the seed (pardon the pun) of our discontentment and mistrust. If the pre-sin Eve were to be transported into our time and place, she would be the Stepford-like woman who has it all. The great job as an horticulturalist/zookeeper, the perfect husband, a Bear Grylls/ Dr. Phil hybrid who can do manly things but also puts the toilet seat down and brings her breakfast in bed. She would be muffin-top free and have hair that always looked windswept but in a good way. And yet she wanted more. More of what? It wasn't more fruit. She had a whole orchard at her disposal. No, that day in Eden, Satan whispered his own desire into Eve's ear and she swallowed it whole; it lodged in her heart where it still blooms today in her daughters. That desire is to be god-like, to be in control, to be the one who sets the boundaries and makes all the rules.

So when suffering of both the inconvenient and downright serious variety comes into our lives, the thorns of that blossom prick our hearts and poison our minds. Our hearts cry out that we must be unloved and forgotten. Our minds give birth to thoughts of bitterness and envy. Who does God think He is, bringing us to our knees with cellulite or unemployment or loneliness or disease?

Well, He thinks He's God. He thinks He is the Creator of all that we see and so much more. The question isn't who does He think He is but who do we think *we* are? We call ourselves His children yet when He treats us like His own, we cry foul. We aren't the first to experience doubt in the face of discipline (Heb. 12:7–11), but if we are going to identify ourselves as children of God, then we should expect to be disciplined as such. We simply need to look at Jesus, the Son of God, in order to see what we can expect as part of God's family. No bed of roses for the Messiah but rather a cradle of dirty straw. No crown of gold for the King of the Jews but rather a crown of thorns. No exalted throne for God's only begotten Son but rather a cross lifted high. So why on earth would we expect to be treated any differently? The suffering in our lives is not a sign of neglect or displeasure but a confirmation that we are His own. And we in turn are called upon to behave as our brother Jesus did, in obedience and submission. We are the creation, the pots in the hands of the master Potter (Isa. 64:8). But despite the number of praise choruses we sing regarding the love and care He shows us, and despite the number of times He has shown Himself faithful in the past, when suffering jumps out from behind the couch, all too often we panic. We are such temporal creatures, shackled to our immediate circumstances like a couple of chain-gang members. The urgency of our pain and fear drives out all thought of what has come before and what has yet to come.

Having carried and delivered four children into this world has taught me the tendency of pain to peel back the layers, leaving our inner core exposed for all to see. Despite my wish to the contrary, my four beloved blessings were not found in a dew-covered cabbage patch or delivered, diapered and dolled up via stork mail. I grew these four people, piece by piece, pound by pound. That part wasn't so bad. Sure, there were the extra trips to the bathroom, the strange cravings and more elastic waist pants than are good for the ego, but all these small sacrifices are dwarfed when it comes to extracting these bundles of joy from their temporary housing unit. While I mentally envision myself as the serene-in-the-eye-of-the-storm kind of gal, childbirth has brought me to the painful realization that I am, in reality, more of the screaming-words-that-would-make-sailors-blush type.

While I may have waddled into the doctor's office each month all smiles and sweetness, there is no faking it in labor and delivery. Once in the grip of pain so terrible I felt certain I would die from it, a whole lot more than my birth canal was on display for all to see. And it isn't just physical pain that has this varnish scraping effect. I find it easy to appear all churchy and nice when the sun is shining, the laundry is neatly folded, and my hair is having a good day. But trap me in a minivan that smells like last week's lunch box on a rainy day, with a hat pulled low to hide the rat's nest someone cruelly constructed atop my head, and watch out. And that's just a bad day, a hiccup along the road of my life. What happens when money is tight and bills need paying? Or when one of my parents gets a grim diagnosis? Or when any one of the million other hardships I fear might be hiding under the bed decides to crawl under the covers and say hello? Where does that perky, nice girl go then? She vanishes like mist and leaves grouchy, bitter me in her place.

So why does God bring these hiccups and monsters into our lives if all they do is make us feel bad about ourselves and make us question whether or not He cares? Why doesn't He simply shower us with sunshine? The answer to that goes back to giving birth. In order to bring forth the greatest blessings in my life, save Jesus and my hubby, I had to voluntarily enter a room labeled "labor and delivery." I suppose given the choice at the time I might have been tempted to go back, to reverse course, and head for the hills. But were that possible, I would have done so empty-handed. In order to get the blessings, I first had to do the labor. For it is through the pain and the blood that I was delivered.

Between my third and fourth pregnancies, my husband and I experienced the sorrow of a miscarriage. Though we had three great kids at home and every hope of having another, the heartbreak of this lost life cut deep. Since we knew the baby had died but I had not miscarried on my own, the doctor recommended a D&C. We traveled to the hospital that had meant such joy in the past but that day brought only grief. I was put under general anesthesia so there was no pain, no desperate cries for relief. And when I woke up, I was empty. But there was no new life to celebrate. If in that moment I had been given the choice, I would have gladly chosen the pain in order to experience the joy. And when I safely delivered our son Andrew into this world almost one year later, I was glad for the pain that brought new life. Though the pain seems unnatural because, frankly, it is quite unpleasant (gross understatement), the pain of childbirth is the way we bring forth new creations. The pain of our labor is one price we pay for our children's lives.

This is true of our spiritual labor too. But the amazing thing is that the labor has already been done for us. When Jesus groaned and suffered on the cross, He was bringing us out of death and slavery; He was paying for our lives with His own. Whatever pain we suffer here is just the extraction of our new selves from the old. The pain is real and certainly nothing to joke about, but it is fleeting and simply part of the process of giving birth to our new nature. It may hurt like heck, but it will pass. And in our agony, we are not alone. Because He suffered, we can cry out for relief and be heard. It may not stop the pain but it will give us the strength to carry on. We can grab tight to Christ and say, "Don't leave me!" and He never will. He knows our pain and will help to see us through. And when the pain is over, we will sigh and surrender into everlasting rest. We will be delivered. Then we will hear the silence singing and know that it is love.

Chapter Four

Chaotic House on the Prairie

*I am beginning to learn that it is the sweet, simple
things of life which are the real ones after all.*

—Laura Ingalls Wilder, author of
Little House on the Prairie

Imagine *Indiana Jones and the Temple of Doom*. Wait; is
that the creepy one where they are forced to eat eyeballs
and monkey brains? I hate that one. Okay, imagine *Raiders
of the Lost Ark*. Without all the melting-faced Nazis. Think
Harrison Ford, only without the whip and the cool hat.
And he's a she. And instead of a cool gang of sidekicks and
beautiful love interests, this whipless, hatless female version

of Indy is carting around four small kids. Did I mention they aren't exploring archeological sites or being chased by bad guys wearing black leather and swastikas? Instead, they are wheeling through a grocery store at half past nap time trying to find a cereal that everyone likes and figure out how much 3/$5 is when you are only buying two. I suppose, superficially speaking, they don't have much in common, that fictitious archeologist-turned-defender-of-truth and this all-too-real woman-turned-seeker-of-a-potty-break-and-a-bargain. His is a life of excitement and danger, traveling to the far corners of the world in order to uncover lost artifacts. Hers is a life of monotony and repetition, traveling to the far corners of the minivan in order to discover someone's lost math homework. But there are similarities, if one is looking past the superficial differences of gender, occupation, and lifestyle. (Okay, maybe those things aren't exactly superficial.) At heart, they are both seeking something—something of lasting and historical significance. Their methodologies may differ, but in the end, they are both seekers of great treasure.

One of the first things people like to do when babies are born is to carefully study the newborn infant's face in order to ascertain whose characteristics, the mother's or father's, are more strongly represented. I confess to having done this with each of my kids, all the while realizing that it is an exercise in futility. Though they are sweet and wonderful, babies are, for the most part, rather generic in appearance, and the person who claims to truly discern distinct features in the face of a newborn is either an expert in facial recognition or lying. This isn't a personal insult to all infants. Their faces have just been squeezed through a canal the diameter of a tailpipe. Obviously some allowances have to be made as they adjust to life outside the womb. It isn't until kids get a little older that one is able to see the combined characteristics of Mom and Dad in the various aspects of the human face. And this isn't just true of physical features. For better and, unfortunately, for worse, children inherit a lot more than just their mother's eyes or their dad's forehead. Mom's sense of humor (and stubbornness) along with Dad's athleticism (and dislike of tomatoes) are along for the genetic train ride as well.

This shared gene pool brings many great joys in life. Being like other people can give you a deep sense of belonging and security. When I was younger, I would search through pictures of my parents as children, trying to trace my smile or posture. As offspring, we spend the first part of our lives as DNA detectives, examining all the ways in which we are similar to and dissimilar from our parents and siblings. Then we have our own kids and start all over with them. As a parent, it can be a thrill to see yourself reflected in the face or personality of another. I stress the word "can." There are other times when the feeling is one of humiliation and sadness rather than pride and joy. Often these times come not when I see the weaknesses I have passed on to my children but when their weaknesses highlight my own.

Even as I lecture my children on the errors of their ways, I become more aware of my own shortcomings. I whine about their whining. I am impatient with their impatience. I may be more skilled in disguising my lack of self-control or selfishness, but it's there all the same.

At no time is the "mule-headed" gene, which runs so deep in my family, more apparent than when we are required to leave the house as a unit. Sure we have our struggles at home or when trying to send one or two of us out the door. But there is something about the additional pressure of time constraint (not to mention all of us trying to brush our teeth at the same time) that creates an atmosphere in which we are all ticking time bombs waiting to be triggered. Trying to harness six wills in a singular direction at the same time feels like a Herculean feat. Somewhere in between searching for shoes and spitting on cowlicks that refuse to stay down, I begin to question the importance of leaving the house at all. My desire to participate in any elective outings such as story hours and playdates at the park has definitely decreased significantly with each addition to our brood.

We are a society of endless social possibilities. Trying to pick and choose what you will participate in and who you will keep up with is like trying to drink from a fire hose. You are knocked to your feet by the sheer volume and though soaking wet, you are more than likely still thirsty. With seemingly limitless opportunities for interaction through small groups, Facebook, online communities, Bible studies and more, how do we practice discernment and simplicity when it comes to our social lives as individuals and as families? How do we minimize the amount of avoidable conflict that arises from overbooking our social calendars? How do we overcome our own selfish desires in order to serve to others without becoming a doormat for the others' selfish desires?

So much of the tension that arises in any relationship, like the tension of the Spiegel family trying to get out the door on time, is not a matter of overt sin but rather a battle of wills. This will-induced conflict is one of the reasons we are more likely to have conflict with those closest to us. We aren't embarrassed to demand that we get our own way. When we argue with our parents or siblings, become irritated with our roommates or spouses, many times it isn't because one of us has committed some great moral misstep. Rather it is because they won't do what we want them to do or vice versa. We would like to think that the conflicts we face feature us as the defender of the good, ready to slay evil in the hearts of those around us. However, if we are looking to purge evil from the world, most of the time we need not search any further than our own selfish hearts.

My selfish heart is too often revealed when it comes to dragging my children around like four pieces of luggage I have been burdened with rather than four individuals with needs and opinions of their own. There have been seasons of homeschooling and babies when I have hunkered down at home like I was sitting out an air raid or a large scale nuclear attack; only leaving to resupply and for the occasional breath of fresh air. I was willing to forego the pleasures of this world for the sake of lesson planning and sleep schedules. But as those seasons passed, like a compulsive gambler who can't resist the draw of the casino, I would commit myself to completely unnecessary activities in the name of educational enrichment and enjoyment that were neither particularly educational nor enjoyable for anyone. Most of what my kids learn from these experiences is to duck and head for cover when Mom is trying to load the car. I throw my bag over my shoulder like a Navy Seal straps on extra ammo, armed with more fruit snacks, hand sanitizer, and water bottles than you can shake a stick at. Get in my way at your own peril.

In brief moments of clarity somewhere between grabbing granola bars and trying to locate my keys, I see that too many times the reason this is all so stressful is *my* crusader mentality and not any willful disobedience on my children's part. *I* want to get out of the house. *I* want to get to story hour so I can talk with *my* friends. Rather than considering what is best for us as a whole, I demand that everyone do things my way. My cause is probably just—going to church, getting to school on time—but surely there is a better way to encourage submission than by the sword.

And of course, this infantile behavior is not limited to my interactions with my children. Just ask anyone who has tried to convince me to go to a restaurant I didn't like or talk me out of an unnecessary and labor intensive activity. The irony is that many events my children are being forcibly marched to are supposedly for them. Or I force friends to eat at places I love, putting aside their own personal tastes and preferences. I have more than once panicked that my children will be utter failures later in life if I don't take them to at least one or two mind-enriching activities a week. Half the time they don't want to go but fear puts a fire in my belly like no other and so off we go in a whirl-wind of confusion. They would have been content to stay home and play board games.

It's sad that so much of the chaos of our lives is created not by the basic demands of our primary responsibilities but our refusal to stand against the cultural dictates that demand that every moment of our lives be filled with activ-ity. The damage done when our self-created stress explodes in impatience and a frenzied attitude could never be justi-fied by any benefits that we or others might receive from "Crafting 101" or "Bowling for Jesus."

Often my joining seems to be motivated more by a desire not to miss something rather than a desire to actually engage in the activity. And when I know that the next day my friends' blogs will be full of carefully selected pictures that make a movie night seem like the social event of the season, it's hard to say no. I often have to employ my ego-protecting armor in order to go blog surfing and not walk away feeling like a social pariah. "What!? I wasn't invited to the expert-knitting-for-women-in-their-twenties sauer-kraut party last night?" Never mind that I don't knit, I'm not in my twenties, and I hate sauerkraut. Here is where I give myself the following lecture (I try to make it a mental lecture, but there are occasions when I am required to speak the words out loud as I sometimes try to ignore myself): *Last night, you had a great night at home with the hubby and kids. While the expert knitters were having a ball eating sauer-kraut and purl stitching themselves into a frenzy of wooly bliss, you were eating ice cream cones and reading bedtime stories. You like ice cream. You like bedtime stories. It will all be okay.* The thrill of slowing down long enough to figure out what it is I enjoy doing or what I feel called to do has come to me late in life, but I'm learning.

Several years ago Jim and I had the opportunity to visit England over spring break. Our time was limited, and, as unashamed Anglophiles, we wanted to take in as much as possible. We hopped off the plane and hit the ground running, or more accurately, hit the train snoring. True, I finally got to see my beloved Bath (the setting of several Jane Austen novels), but most of the pictures from that leg of our trip feature Jim asleep atop a double-decker red bus. Fortunately for me I am the photographer of the family and therefore none of the pictures captured my whining about how tired and hungry I was. I am sure I heard more than one Brit whisper "Crazy Americans" as we hurried by. Our favorite memory from the entire trip, other than an unfor-gettable personal tour of Liverpool and all things Beatles, was the time we spent puttering around with friends in their small village. That trip brought home the lesson that less is often more, in travel as well as everyday life.

Just when I think it is safe, however, to curl up in the cozy, safe cocoon of my family compound, I find myself drifting to the other extreme. Like Odysseus trying to stay clear of Scylla on the one hand and Charybdis on the other, I have difficulty keeping away from overcommitment without becoming lazy and complacent. When the phone rings and I don't want to answer, is it because I think that right now it is more important for me to finish Maggie's language arts lesson or is it because I really don't want to lay aside my personal agenda in order to listen to someone else?

There are times when letting it go to voice mail isn't a bad option. You have to prioritize, but sometimes the motives behind our priorities can get a little murky. Are you skipping Bible study because you really need to study and go to bed early, or because you fear the accountability of confession? Are you a no-show at the committee meeting because you want to spend some quality time with the fam or because you want to be in sweatpants by nine? For me, it is a discipline to prioritize interacting with others rather than constantly retreating inside of myself. Getting too close to others can feel threatening, as if I will expose all my failings, despite the fact that they know them already! For others I know, the discipline is to set aside time when they aren't interacting or socializing and learn to be content with solitude. Being alone with your thoughts can sometimes be as revealing as sharing them with others.

Whichever discipline you need to practice, it goes back to those battling wills again. Only this time the will that we are battling with is our own. It is a symptom of this strange reality of dualism that exists in the heart of each believer. Dual as in there are two natures, the old and new. But also "duel" as in dueling, pistols loaded and drawn to see who will claim victory, the flesh or the spirit. This experience is analogous to physical training. We commit to train for a race or reach a certain goal and yet every morning is a battle to get out of bed, to run up one more hill. Despite knowing the reward of pushing ourselves and despite knowing the self-loathing that comes from hitting snooze and going back to sleep, every day it's the same battle. But each time we make the right choice, whether it be in our physical training or spiritual discipline, we are that much stronger for the next day's struggle.

That doesn't mean the process is pretty. Our life's work is to be just that—work. I want to run into the gates of heaven out of breath and dripping with sweat not because my effort gets me in but because it is the destination I have been running for all along. May our lives reflect the words of the classic film *Chariots of Fire:* "I believe God made me for a purpose . . . and when I run I feel His pleasure." While the film refers to physical running, I think it can be applied to any effort we pursue for the right reasons.[1]

When we are driven to keep going by fleshy fear of being excluded or missing out on an opportunity that won't come around again, we aren't running in the Spirit. We aren't serving out of gratitude but rather being self-serving.

When in doubt, I try to go back to the example of Christ. He, just like us, had a finite amount of time on earth in which to accomplish a great deal. He, just like us, was sent to redeem creation. His work is the basis for our own and was complete and perfect while ours is not, but the purpose behind His work and ours is the same. To establish the kingdom of God. Jesus wasn't friends with everyone. He had a limited number of disciples in whom He invested deeply. He wasn't a snob, though, and often spent time with those whose company He probably did not enjoy or get warm, fuzzy feelings around. He also spent a great deal of time alone, not eating potato chips and watching action movies but rather praying and fasting, recharging for the work ahead. He didn't heal everyone but allowed the Holy Spirit to guide Him and His ministry.

Jesus' life was one of simplicity. Not of ease and not without complexity. But a cloth that is woven of many hundreds of knots all working together to create a pattern of simple beauty, clear and perfect. It was His willingness to die to His own will and live the will of His Father that created this masterpiece of a life.

Too often my life looks more like a jumble of threads, mismatched, hastily tied, and poorly executed. Pulling colors from here and there, I obscure the Creator's intent. I go running after my own will rather than keeping my eyes on the race that has been set before me. If I will only slow down and refer to the pattern, everything will turn out beautifully.

After years of overcommitting and inviting a great deal of unnecessary stress into my life as well as that of my family, I have learned to ask myself a few questions before making a commitment. Maybe these questions will help you as you strive for simplicity in your own life:

1. Do I actually want to do this activity? This doesn't mean that you only have to do those things you enjoy. I don't enjoy paying our mortgage, but I am fairly certain that is not a legitimate excuse not to do so. But there are plenty of times I have agreed to completely optional activities for me or the kids only to realize we don't like doing the activity. Lots of my friends like to go shopping together. Me? Not so much. I have learned to meet them for dinner since eating is something I really enjoy doing. Think about what you like to do and don't talk yourself into something for fear of being left out. That being said, it's important to try different things. Push yourself out of your comfort zone and you may surprise yourself. If you hate it, you will know not to pick up the phone the next time your friend is organizing a skydiving day o' fun.

2. How will my making this commitment impact my most important responsibilities? Unless you are a hermit, living on a hillside alone and completely self-sufficient, the choices you make affect other people. It's unavoidable. Sometimes the ends justify the means and sometimes they don't. My family has lived much less structured lives in the months that I have been writing this book. I have sometimes chosen time together over strict bedtimes and sanity over well-balanced meals. Overall, I think we have weathered it pretty well. But there are other times when I did something because I was afraid of being looked down on or in order to receive great recognition by those on the outside, all the while neglecting my responsibilities at home and being unkind to my family to boot. We only have so much time and energy to give, and our primary responsibilities should get first dibs.

3. What would those who know me best tell me to do? Everything I have learned about the art of discerning priorities and maintaining simplicity in my life, I learned from my husband. I hate it because I love to say yes to things, but he has been right too many times to be ignored. Now, before I sign on the dotted line, I either consult him or do my best to anticipate his response. "Honey, should I sign the kids up for goat herding lessons at a farm forty-five minutes a way? They are really expensive, the goats bite, and it's a six-month commitment?" I would seriously have to think this one through if it weren't for Jim. Sad, but true.

Once, when accused of not being the man he once was, Indiana Jones replied, "It's not the years, honey. It's the mileage." Indiana realizes that it isn't just how old something is but what it has been through in those years that affect its condition. All his discoveries and adventures have left him altered, marked by the experience. Perhaps his mileage left him worse for wear. But not so for our female Indy. She has had fewer close calls or escapes from death, nevertheless the miles have changed her as well. She, too, has been marked by the journey, though her scars might not be as visible as his. Just like Professor Jones, she has found her treasure, though it is unlikely to bring her either fame or fortune. Unlike Jones, she hasn't found it trotting the globe, searching in caves or ancient ruins. She has searched for great treasure in the slow-moving waters and been greatly rewarded for her quest.

Chapter Five

Greater Expectations

*Pause you who read this, and think for a moment
of the long chain of iron or gold, of thorns or flowers,
that would never have bound you, but for the
formation of the first link on one memorable day.*
—Charles Dickens, *Great Expectations*

Like a wounded animal looking for a place to hide, I sit, crying tears of regret and frustration. Of course, I feel a bit silly, a grown woman huddled in my kitchen pantry, but sometimes a girl needs a bit of privacy. As children run and play obliviously outside my hiding place, I mumble words of repentance under my breath. I pray for strength as I feebly attempt to defeat my enemy.

My adversary isn't an in-your-face-and-wears-a-creepy-mask enemy. She's a smiles-sweetly-holds-a-basket-of-cookies-in-one-hand-and-a-verbal-dagger-in-the-other sort of enemy. She coats her lies in sugar and spice, making them easier to swallow as they turn to poison and slowly kill you from the inside. I am hunted by her, tortured by her when found. She pretends to be my friend, encouraging me to set goals she knows I can't achieve. When I fail, she mocks my failure and laughs at my humiliation. I have managed to elude her for a time, but somehow she always finds me. I have tried to make peace with her. I have tried to shun her but she always returns. She creates to-do lists a mile long and Googles Bible reading programs that would make the most devoted monk shudder.

She is drowning me in a sea of high expectations. She is carefully paving my way to hell with the best of intentions. I hear her thoughts in my head and even see her in the mirror. Because this mortal enemy of mine is me.

I am a list maker extraordinaire. When faced with an outing with the kids or an expedition with friends, I can reach a level of preparedness that would make the Boy Scouts proud and potentially win a medal from Homeland Security. In fact, list making and advance planning are my security. I like to know what to expect and then make a plan based on those expectations. My husband would say it's a control thing and of course he would be right, darn him and his insights.

There is so much that I can't control in this life: whether or not my hair will look windswept and carefree or wind-tangled and couldn't-care-less; whether my children will play harmoniously while I catch up with a friend or tear one another's eyeballs out over the most trivial of disputes; whether my parents will be healthy and active for many years to come or be struck down with disease and disability. But when I set my pen to paper, I am the captain of my own destiny. I can imagine worlds in which errands are done in an efficient and orderly manner, where borrowed books don't mysteriously disappear from the book bag, and where I manage to get everything on my grocery list and manage to stay within budget. In reality, I may only get half of my list accomplished, have library fines out the wazoo, and leave a mile-deep stack of "optional" items behind at checkout. But before any of these unexpected obstacles arise, I can plaster on the biggest of Pollyanna smiles and dream big dreams.

Everyone has lists of expectations and not just of the day-to-day variety. Bucket lists of things we want to see and do, things we want to become in life. These lists can help to propel us into action, but they can also become burdens that slow us down. When it comes to setting expectations for ourselves, how do we walk the fine line between being motivated and being legalistic? How can we pursue excellence out of devotion to our Creator without losing perspective on what the pursuit is all about? What do we do when our list is different from that of our neighbor? How can we accept and encourage one another rather than trying to impose our own standards on others?

In the daily running of my life, I personally find list making an effective way to order my often disorderly thoughts. However romantic the idea of taking things as they come, when flying by the seat of your pants one often ends up exposing one's backside. Lists often, though not always, help me to avoid these metaphorical moonings. Part of growing into your own skin is recognizing the properties and limitations of the materials you are dealing with. I can dream about being the happy-go-lucky, devil-may-care kind of gal but I'm not. I'm the let's-get-organized, devil's-in-the-details kind of gal.

Whichever camp you fall into or if you hover in the no-man's-land somewhere in between, that is how you were created. We could all use some fine-tuning, and the extremes on either end are to be avoided. Go too far in one direction and you are in danger of drowning in the chaos of your life, to be found by rescue parties under an avalanche of missed appointments and unpaid bills. On the other end of the spectrum, you are in danger of becoming a controlling looney woman whose world is reduced to the boundaries of what she can control. Look into the mirror, take stock of your natural tendencies, and give them a big ol' bear hug of acceptance. We must embrace and accept our psychological makeup just as we must make peace with our physical imperfections and play up our natural beauty.

There is a delicate balance between embracing our natures and making excuses for our failures. In Bible studies or among friends, I have found myself admitting sins in a humorous and exaggerated way that mimics confession but is more closely related to dismissal. If I make jokes about snapping at the kids while trying to do my devotions or the busyness that "prevents" me from having meaning-ful times of prayer, then no one can accuse me of being inauthentic. But they can't accuse me of being morally seri-ous either. This is one of the reasons I generally avoid the blogging world. Too often blogs by Christian women fall into two basic categories: Category One is the "authentic" blogger who braggingly blogs about the disarray in her life, the unfolded laundry, the extra pounds she has decided to accept. While I appreciate her honesty and certainly iden-tify with her struggles, maybe we should spend less time being authentic and more time creating order out of chaos. Category Two is the "excellent" blogger who spends every minute of the day enriching the lives of all those around her, alphabetizing her food pantry and developing a cure for leprosy. Again, I appreciate her zest for life, but maybe Miss Category Two needs to go over to Category One's house for a while and then take a nap.

If we put these women in a blender, metaphorically that is, the end product seems to be the perfect balance of honesty and determination. Honesty in that we are fearfully and wonderfully made, loved and accepted by our Maker. Christ died that we might approach the throne of God, as well as our next PTA meeting, without fear of judgment. Category One women encourage us to be honest about our shortcomings and embrace who God has created us to be. But we are also sinful and corrupt and are called to make war with our fleshly nature (Ps. 58:3; 139:14). Without a clear picture of our sinful nature, there is no good news to be found in the gospel. Coming out and admitting our faults and weaknesses can be a great comfort to those with similar struggles. We don't want, however, to give others or ourselves an excuse. We are diseased, but there is a cure, however long the recovery process.

That's where determination comes in. We should strive, through the work of the Holy Spirit, to improve those aspects of our personalities that hinder us from bringing God greater glory. We can do this by first acknowledging our areas of weakness but then going about the business of becoming stronger.

My van is usually messy and I am typically late in arriving at my destination. I hate these things about myself. I want to be the sparkling clean and tidy van girl and follow my father's example of always being early. These are things I can work on and over time change, but I first must acknowledge the need for improvement. I make excuses for the van being dirty. I have reasons why I am not on time. Everyone's car is sometimes a mess and everyone, except my dad, is occasionally late, but I have to be willing to admit that my problem goes beyond the sometimes and occasional. Like an alcoholic who admits it in order to find accountability and not affirmation, I confess so that I can change: My name is Amy and I am a messy van owner and late arriver. Maybe I should start putting "Clean the van" and "Be on time" on my list along with "Buy crickets for the lizard" and "Get a haircut." But then again, there are other, more weighty matters that need to go on that list as well like "Strive to be more loving" and "Forgive others more wholeheartedly."

List making and self-imposed expectations can certainly help us to conquer those daily habits that make life more stressful than it need be, but making spiritual to-do lists can bring more rather than less chaos into my life. These lists which are written in the recesses of my heart are spiritual manifestos that create bondage out of freedom. Having been raised from the death of my sin, I often forge new bonds for myself, a Jacob Marley who should no longer be burdened but continues to carry the chains of my own making. Unlike miserly Marley who is forced to cling-clang his way through the afterlife as punishment for his greedy ways, someone else has loosed my chains and set me free. As the psalmist says, "He brought them out of darkness and the deepest gloom and broke away their chains" (Ps. 107:14). But I daily return to the prison of legalism, looking for scrap metal with which I can imprison myself.

I am certain I am not alone in this insanity. I hear the clanging of Christian women's fettered journeys all around me. We are like the Israelites, freed from the slavery of Egypt, with the dust of the Red Sea still on our feet, crying out to be delivered back into bondage.

Though I would love to attribute the Israelites' desire to return to brick making to heat stroke, I think their attitude, and mine, has less to do with hydration and more to do with our hearts. Looking down the family tree, the root of the problem becomes clear. Once upon a time Adam and Eve stood at the foot of another tree, and there they were faced with a choice: remain free to serve on God's terms or become a slave on their own terms. We all know how that turned out. But despite the obvious stupidity of their choice, we can hardly point a finger. We have been given a choice as well. We have been returned, in part, to the garden through the blood of Jesus, to serve. Yet all too often we choose self-enslavement over God-enslavement. As the serpent coils around us tighter and tighter, we think that we are the ones in control and would rather suffocate in our own sin than breathe freely as we serve Someone beyond our control. We look into the face of God and bite down hard on the apple of rebellion.

This rebellion can take many shapes. Just as Satan has taken the form of a serpent and "masquerades as an angel of light" (2 Cor. 11:14), our defiance is sometimes there for all to see and sometimes more subtly concealed. When we break God's law or reject Christian fellowship in order to pursue our own agenda, that is clearly taking up arms against our Lord. Rather than take our pain and anger to God, who is more than capable of handling it, we take it out on those around us and ultimately on ourselves. Our pride refuses to bend the knee. I have experienced this type of rebellion and all its bleak consequences. There were times when I was so far down in the pit I had dug for myself, I couldn't see daylight. I knew it was there but refused to cry out for help, to admit my weakness. I buried myself alive in sin and shame. Thankfully I did eventually come to my senses and God heard my "six feet under screams," to quote the great "theologian" and pop singer Katy Perry.

In many ways this type of rebellion is easier to confront in our lives because it is more obvious. But what about the times when we cloak ourselves in all the trappings of our faith, all the outward behaviors of the law but inwardly we are spies for the enemy? This spiritual espionage is nothing new. Jesus spent a great deal of time dealing with it during His earthly sojourn. In those days it was the Pharisees, always adding to the law just to prove how many hoops they were able to jump through. Today it is the artificial churchy face version of ourselves that wears her Vacation Bible School answers on her sleeve, ready to whip out a "Great, and how are you doing?" at a moment's notice.

The temptation toward legalism is a strong one. Many are drawn into adding to the law out of a passion to serve God more completely. James tells us that "faith without deeds is dead" (James 2:26). In a desperate effort to prove ourselves alive, we can somehow misplace the gospel we are attempting to prove we believe in. It's like becoming so engrossed in planning the perfect party that you fail to notice the guest of honor is missing. But whatever your motives are, legalism is poison to the soul and will ultimately kill faith. If we write our own law, then it is ourselves we are serving and not God. Making the straight and narrow path even more narrow through legalism is the same as forsaking the way altogether. While immoral behavior may be a rejection of God's commands, legalism is the rejection of God's grace. The fruit we bear in our lives should blossom out of a deep trust in God's provision, not an attempt to repay the great debt we owe.

This should come as a great relief. So why is the temptation to legalism so great? Because once we unconditionally surrender to the mercy of God, more surrendering lies ahead. We can't just drop our sins at the foot of the cross like yesterday's garbage and go our merry way. If we want Him to take our sin, then He has to take our hearts as well. He has to take all our future plans, hopes, and desires. He has to take our jobs, our spouse, and our children. This is where we surrender our pens to Him so that He may write the lists of His expectations on our heart. His lists don't include making the bed and going to the grocery. They don't even include feeding the poor or clothing the naked, though these might be the natural consequences of what He writes there. His expectations are so much greater than our own. They are "love the Lord your God with all your heart, your mind and soul and love your neighbor as yourself." Jesus isn't looking to be penciled in to your busy schedule of activities. He is looking to take over your entire calendar.

This makes Jesus sound a bit greedy but, of course, He isn't. He takes it all because it is already His. We might like to think that we control all those things but, of course, we don't. By surrendering these "possessions," we simply acknowledge His rightful ownership. In return He either gives them back to us for our enjoyment or gives us something better in return. This enjoyment is so much greater now that we no longer have to fear for the ultimate care of these things. We play our part as caregiver but with the knowledge that if the job is taken away, it is because the owner of our soul has something else in mind. Something harder, perhaps, but always, in the end, something better. Or He might leave some desire unfulfilled so that we can learn to cling to Him more closely. Again, this isn't easy but if we believe and take that leap of faith, He is always there to catch us before we hit the ground. Our unfulfilled desires are replaced with a great understanding of His care, which seems like a pretty good trade.

The Bible is full of people who gave up their own expectations and were given much greater ones in return. Sarah never expected to be a barren woman transformed into a rejoicing mother. Moses never expected to be an outcast turned deliverer. Saul never expected to be a persecutor turned into the apostle Paul, champion of Christian faith.

In my life I have had a little bit of both the enjoying and the withholding. A year or so after the birth of our first child, I got out my to-do list and wrote "Have another baby." It truly never crossed my mind that two years later that list would sit dusty and forlorn, still not crossed off, still no bun in the oven. One day, an older, wiser friend told me that our children are God's children, not our own. And that means that if He chooses not to give them to us, that is His business. And if He does choose to bring them into this world, then their life hereafter is His business as well. I would be well off to remember this as I raised the child I had and as I prayed for more. Not long after, I rejoiced in the knowledge that I was pregnant, but I never forgot my friends words of wisdom. That same precious child was very sick once and I forced myself to claim him not for myself but for my Lord and Savior and His purposes. I might have certain expectations for that child and my other three regarding their moral development, their futures, and so on. But each day I must force myself to claim them not for myself but for my Lord's purposes and will.

When I despair over my own slow moral development, I am reminded that I am God's child as well. He has called me "according to his purpose" (Rom. 8:28) and His purpose will not fail. I may stumble. I may fall. But if I am in Him, I will not fail. His work in me will be completed one day (Phil. 1:6). When I attempt to take life not from its true source—my Father's will and purpose—but my own, the results are not pretty. Like some mad Frankensteinian scientist, I frantically create the person I think I should be. I look at those whom I admire and respect not with appreciation for God's work in their lives, but with green eyes of envy seeking to acquire what is not mine. I piece together all these enviable attributes and sew them on, not in the spirit but in the flesh. The result is not the new creation I am called to be but a hideous monster that roars in frustration and despair. I create not a better version of myself but an enemy to my very soul.

Time and time again I realize the futility of playing spiritual dress-up. I can't write out spiritual goals in the same way that I write out a list for printer ink and new underwear, as if closeness to God or increased patience were merely items in a store that we can acquire for the right price. Blood is what is required to obtain what I desire but not my own. If I want to see myself transformed spiritually I must first take off—through confession and repentance—all the stolen parts in which I have covered myself. I must confess the ways in which I have counterfeited spiritual growth and repent of my envious ways. Only then can I humbly request that God work through me as He wills. Through prayer and the study of His Word, my creation will be brought to life.

Though I doubt Jesus sat, scroll in hand, and made a to-do list for Himself, His life was a well-planned life. Long before He took human form, His earthly course of action was determined. He checked off each task through the power of the Holy Spirit as He accomplished what was set before Him. In His final hours this side of the cross, He said, "Not my will but yours be done," just as He had said every day of His life. But it *was* His will because He and the Father had the same plan. He thought not of His own soul, but the souls of all mankind trapped in the slavery of sin and death. He knew that to surrender was not to lose but to win; to hang His head in death was the way to rise again in life eternal.

Jesus knew that to be enslaved to God was to find true freedom. His victory is mine and I must claim it as my own. My lists and plans need not include any other item than to follow in His footsteps, wherever that might lead.

I'm back in the pantry, my homemade confessional of sorts. The kids are still playing and I am still crying. I have come not to hide but to be seen. I know my enemy and she is me. And so I have come to surrender and plea for mercy.

I know that my path to glory is often blocked with obstacles of my own making. And so I have come to pray for their removal.

I know that there is a to-do list written by the hand of God just for me. And so I have come that I might lay aside my own list and accept His.

I will be back tomorrow to repeat the whole process again. It will be on my list underneath buying crickets for the lizard and getting a haircut. I will bend the knee again and again and say, "Not my will but Yours" until the list is finished. I look forward to the day of its completion with the greatest of expectations. The day when I am no longer my own worst enemy.

Chapter Six

Pride and Providence

Mr. Wickham is blessed with such happy manners as may ensure his making friends—whether he may be equally capable of retaining them, is less certain.

—Jane Austen, *Pride and Prejudice*

It happens all over the country, perhaps even all over the world. Small groups of women gather in coffee shops and backyards, around the neighborhood swimming pool, and on side-by-side treadmills in the gym. They carefully strike a tone balanced somewhere between the casual and confidential. They send out discreet feelers while trying not to come across as too eager.

No, these women aren't discussing the future of the housing market or the fate of the Middle East peace talks. They are negotiating the terms for next year's carpool. These talks start about the beginning of August, when baseball season is finally over, when everyone has returned from summer vacations and their sunburns have finally mellowed into a lovely shade of beef jerky. The slow pace of summer peels away like the skin off our backs and is replaced by an undercurrent of tension and fear.

Being included is a sure sign that you are valued even if only for the extra space in the back of your minivan. To be excluded is like being chosen last for dodge ball or going to the prom with your cousin. Whether a mother of school-aged children or not, if you are a woman and don't live a life of complete solitude, you have experienced this in some form. Waiting to get the invitation for the sleepover "everyone" is going to; overhearing weekend plans among roommates that don't include you; spotting your favorite married friends out with another couple. It is a bitter irony that friendship, something that brings such great joy, can also be the source of such deep sorrow. To quote the great sage who is my mother-in-law, "Friendships between women are tenuous at best." Suddenly solitary confinement doesn't sound so bad after all.

In our kitchen we have a large set of windows overlooking our quiet (when the motorcycles aren't in season), tree-lined street. I spend a great deal of the day standing, looking out these windows, as I am making dinner, washing dishes, and doing a hundred other small daily tasks. It's strange that such a beautiful view can, on occasion, inspire sorrow rather than joy, envy rather than gratitude. You see, two of my good friends, and their swarm of kids with whom my swarm of kids greatly enjoy playing, live almost directly across from these windows and right next to each other. Between us is a church parking lot that functions as a demilitarized zone for the swarm, their roller blades, bikes, and scooters. It is rare that a day passes without me watching one of the kids dash across the street, barely avoiding being struck by a car, while running off to see if someone can play.

What a blessing, right? Funny how human beings have a talent for taking every blessing and twisting it into a curse. I know that James tells us that fresh and salt water cannot come from the same source (James 3:11), but when it comes to female friendship, I beg to differ. The same spring that delivers soul-bolstering laughter and encouragement can also bubble over with soul-crushing resentment and frustration. While I often smile as I watch my kids' mad dash toward friendship, there are other times, more often than I care to admit, that I stand on tiptoe to make sure I'm not being left out of anything fun. I realize this puts my maturity level on a par with that of a middle schooler. You can take the girl out of the cafeteria, but you can't take the *oh-crabapples-I-don't-have-anyone-to-sit-with* experience out of the girl. If I am humble enough to admit this to any one of the women in my acquaintance, I imagine most of them would quickly confess to feeling the same way.

I live in a unique environment when it comes to female friendships. Between the smallness of our town and the tight-knit nature of Jim's work environment, the overlap of school, community, sports for the kids, work, and friends can sometimes resemble an inbred family tree with one big trunk and very few branches. I suppose we are one of those off-shooting branches in that we go to a church where few other Taylor folks attend and live in a nearby town rather than in the shadow of the university. This has provided a little breathing space for Jim and me who, by nature, lean more toward the introverted than the extroverted side of the social spectrum. We like people, but we also like to have our space. At least most of the time. But sometimes all that space gets a little lonely for this girl. I find myself straining to see what is happening on the other side of the fence where all that green grass is growing.

I've found that if not treated with a large dose of gratitude for all the vegetation growing on this side of the fence, weeds of discontentment can set down deep roots that choke out the healthy and good. One of the best weed killers I have found is the truth. The truth about how I came to be planted where I am and not in rockier soil; the truth about all the blessings I derive from here rather than somewhere else.

I am a devout believer in the all-guiding hand of God's providential work. I see this not only in Scripture but in the unfolding of personal events of my own life. As the psalmist says, "All the days ordained for me were written in your book before one of them came to be" (Ps. 139:16). Like the story of Theseus who conquered the Labyrinth simply by following a ball of yarn, I can escape the dangers of ingratitude and false thinking by following the chain of events that have led me to be in this place and time. When I choose to dwell on feeling excluded from this relationship or that event, it is like choosing to let go of that guiding thread and wander off into the darkness. But when I see myself being led in one direction rather than another, being led by God's design, I find myself coming out of the maze of my ungrateful thoughts. If Joseph can look into the eyes of his lying and disloyal brothers and say, "You meant this for evil but God used it for good," who am I to whine about my life circumstances? By tracing back the steps that have led me here, I can rest assured that this is where I am supposed to be.

When our daughter was born, Jim and I had to accept the fact that we were no longer going to be able to function as a family without a larger vehicle. However we twisted and rearranged, our midsized backseat was not going to accommodate three car seats. We entertained fantasies of being among the uber-hip who shun the conventional minivan and scoot around town in an old Volvo station wagon, rear-facing third seat included. Our limited budget and two kids who are prone to carsickness forced us to abandon our Volvo dreams and start looking for a minivan we could afford. It was summer and two weeks of visiting family and thirty hours of driving three across the backseat was looming. The day before we were to leave, we got the call. A friend of my parents had found us a van. There was a little issue with the automatic doors, but otherwise it was a great find. We offered up loud thanksgiving at being spared the torture of cramming everyone into the back and headed south, confident in God's provision. I have to remind myself of that confidence every time I spend ten minutes trying to resolve that "little door problem" or when I have to reassure a friend that the check engine light is always on or when a child waves to me from the back of a Volvo, facing the rear and not looking the least bit carsick.

I am a TLC addict and when given the chance will watch *What Not to Wear* episodes until I can't tell a drop waist from an empire. It's amazing to see fashion disasters transformed into fashionistas. Life as a believer is a bit like that. We start out as a moral disaster and in the end are changed into something beautiful. Only our process is a very slow one. Sometimes we think we know what looks good on us, but in reality it is very unflattering. Rather than playing up our strengths, the old familiar habits or things we most long for highlight our flaws. You might say we want a makeover, but unless we are willing to put ourselves in the hands of the Designer, we will never be transformed.

Our views on friendship can be one such "problem area." We might try to disguise our longing for affirmation by dressing it up in language about the "body of Christ" when what we really are looking for is a place where we feel completely comfortable. Though we might talk about wanting to serve and support others, what we are really looking for is others who will serve and support us. And if they think we are funny, like our cooking, and greatly admire our parenting skill, that's great too. We may say we want an outfit that is right for us, but the truth is we want to wear our sweatpants and look good too. We are not looking for community; we are looking for an entourage.

It is difficult to accept God's leading in the area of friendships because it seems like an area where a little hedonism is socially acceptable. You don't hear too many people going out to look for friends among those with whom they have nothing in common or don't find particularly interesting. We are supposed to like our friends, right? Certainly I think God has created us to be social beings and to that extent He wants us to enjoy the same type of fellowship that the Father, Son, and Holy Spirit enjoy. The Holy Trinity doesn't merely tolerate each other. They are made perfect and complete by Their relationship. As appealing as the idea of arranged marriage is to me as a parent, when looking for a spouse, for ourselves or others, we certainly don't overlook difference in temperament or interests that might make two people less compatible. So, yes, we should like our friends, but that doesn't mean they shouldn't challenge and stretch us. I like to work out, but that doesn't mean it isn't work. If it didn't make me sweaty and maybe even sore the next day, it probably wasn't much of a workout.

The same is true for our friends. We should have to put up with them sometimes as a way of practicing the discipline of patience. We should also remember that they probably find us just as annoying sometimes and in that way practice the discipline of humility. It is through human relationships that so much of our sanctification takes place. If we remember that all of our friends' irritating habits are from the hand of God, then as our friends grate on our nerves or challenge us to reconsider certain positions, it is God's way of polishing us into perfection.

If we need an example of someone who chose His friends in order to learn greater patience, we need look no further than Jesus. If I am tempted to choose sweatpants friends who are comfortable and easy to be around, Jesus chose camel-hair friends, friends who get under your skin and are very irritating. What an entourage He had! The disciples were not exactly prestige friends, and I'm sure they weren't in the elite carpool. Christ had something to offer them, not the other way around. He chose friends who needed a friend. He could have chosen just to hang out at the temple with the leaders and thinkers of the day. He and John the Baptist could have gone on a revival tour together. Certainly Jesus spoke to large crowds and interacted with people of influence and power. But in the end, the man who changed the world forever did so through relationships. He formed the ultimate men's Bible study group and not only impacted the lives of those in attendance but the entire history of our planet. He cared little for appearances and focused on all of His friends' needs, while I too often see friends as means to an end, accessories I can pull out to make myself look better. What would my friendships look like if I thought of them as Jesus did rather than as commodities bringing me greater satisfaction and comfort in life?

Ultimately the commodification of friendship is not only wrong but self-defeating. Thinking only of myself just magnifies each perceived slight, which makes me think about myself more, and so on. The irony is that when I die to self and let go of my firm grip on self-interest, it is in that moment I find peace. When I am only looking out for myself, I am all I see. This experience is a bit like looking too closely at one's reflection in the glare of the dressing room mirror. Absolutely no good can come of it.

Often I look out for myself when all the while I should be looking out for opportunities to serve. The contentment that I feel in the presence of others does not come from thinking about myself. It's when I look to the needs of others that I cure my loneliness. The isolation Jesus experienced every day of His life on earth wasn't cured by gathering to Himself the best and the brightest. It was through His ultimate sacrifice for our sake that He restored fellowship with His Father, for Himself as well as for us (Phil. 2:5–11). The community of heaven awaits me if I am willing to lay down my life. God placed me in front of a window looking out, not in front of a mirror looking in.

A little self-reflection isn't a bad thing, of course. If you are an introvert, don't be ashamed. Come join me in the corner over here, and we can enjoy not talking to one another. Being alone gives you time to process and think through things. Jesus spent time with His apostles, but He also went His own way on a regular basis and enjoyed times of solitude. Besides, I never leave a social gathering without having said something I regret, so I look at time to myself as the only time, other than when I am sleeping, in which I manage not to offend someone. For some of us, time spent alone is critical to being a friend; without it we are grumpy and unpleasant. For others, it is a discipline to be practiced and endured. Whichever the case might be, balancing the time you spend with and without people is crucial for mental health.

Having diversity in your friendships is also important. I love having friends that look at the world in a very different way than I do. It keeps me on my toes and prevents me from becoming too entrenched in my own political, social, or theological assumptions. I also like having friends who are at a different life stage than I am. Those who are a bit farther down the road than I can offer great advice and much-needed perspective. Hopefully I can do the same for those who haven't reached my phase of life yet. My older friends teach me to appreciate this stage because it won't last forever and my younger friends remind me to cherish every moment. To me, one of the greatest missteps of modern American evangelical church has been the segregating of the church by age group. We have much to learn from one another, and it is sad that this diversity of perspective is undervalued by so many churches.

Just having friends isn't enough, however. Our

friendships should be ones that are pleasing to God and edifying to us as well as our friends. Someone once said that "Great minds discuss ideas, average minds discuss events, and small minds discuss people." I have taken this as a personal challenge because it is so easy to be lazy and just talk about who did what and so on. These discussions aren't necessarily mean-spirited, but they are rarely mind-improving. I am most guilty of this with my husband who is also my closest friend. As a professional philosopher, he gets home from work and he is full of ideas and discussion-worthy issues. Instead of rousing myself from the mental lethargy of full-time childcare and housework, I prattle on about the events of the day (not world events, mind you, but which-kid-got-sent-to-timeout and what-funny-thing-another-kid-said events). Perhaps I throw in a few reminders about upcoming obligations and then settle down to read a book or watch a movie. Maybe I ask him about his day but probably from two rooms away with the noise of children filling the intervening space. Hardly an inquiry that would encourage intellectually stimulating conversation.

Good conversations don't just require a commitment to mind-improving topics. They require a commitment of time and energy. Can you imagine how boring most of the disciples' conversations were to Jesus? Here is the Son of God, full of the knowledge of the universe, and Peter is telling Him about all the good fishing spots on the Sea of Galilee or John is asking Him to explain the meaning of a parable just one more time. It's worse than Einstein being stuck as a preschool teacher. But I am sure Jesus took the time to listen and re-explain, because Jesus is a perfect friend. As the old hymn asks, "Can we find a friend so faithful who will all our sorrows bear?" Just as He listened to Peter's boring fish stories, He stands ready to listen to our laundry list of complaints and frustrations. He is ever-ready if we will only take the time to "take it to the Lord in prayer."

Perhaps I will master the political subtleties of carpooling, become an acknowledged "player," one of the inner circle and worthy of being entrusted with someone else's offspring. Perhaps I will be accepted into the NATO of shared driving responsibilities. Or perhaps I will be "not in" and left to fend for myself among the lesser vehicular alliances with less known acronyms like the IBSA Dialogue Forum or the International Black Sea Club. Whatever the case may be, I will drive with confidence knowing that this is the road that has been chosen for me. I will drive in peace knowing that Jesus already has the wheel.

Chapter Seven

She Knew She Was Right

The good and the bad mix themselves so thoroughly in our thoughts, even in our aspirations, that we must look for excellence rather in overcoming evil than in freeing ourselves from its influence.
—Anthony Trollope, *He Knew He Was Right*

The summer after we were married, Jim and I decided to make a trip out West. Two of our greatest acquisitions in the whole wedding registry racket were a two-person tent and a camping stove. So we threw these in the trunk and hit the road with a copy of Homer's *Odyssey*, which we read aloud to one another, and an audio book chronicling the travels of Lewis and Clark. We alternated between spending the night in the wilds of KOA campgrounds and crashing with friends and family who were willing to open their homes (and showers) to us. It was a magical time we often refer to, but looking back I have to shake my head at the complete obliviousness of my younger self. Many of the people we stayed with were meeting me for the first time. These close friends, former students, and relatives of Jim obviously had high expectations regarding the new wife of their much beloved friend, professor, and brother. I think I can safely say that while my love for Jim was clear, my maturity was not always as apparent. One way in which I displayed my lack of discernment was my choice of swimming attire. Being summer, we were often in the pool. I would trot out in my bikini, my tattoo, and navel piercing, not to mention a lot of twenty-three-year-old flesh. Though no one said anything, I am sure there was some mental head-shaking and late-night whispering going on.

The bikini is now gone forever, along with the piercing, but the tattoo is still there as a reminder of past errors in judgment. It gives my children something to marvel at when they occasionally catch a glimpse of it. It also helps me to remember that there are some mistakes we will carry with us for life. They may not all be as obvious as my tattoo, but they are there nonetheless. They shape us, for better and for worse, into who we are today. The decisions we make, those we are proud of, those we are ashamed of, and those that require surgical removal, mark us for life.

Whenever my mom hears my friends and I agonizing over an issue regarding parenting, marriage, or modern life in general, she smiles indulgently and gives us a loving roll of the eyes. Patient woman that she is, she has spent hours listening to me wrestle with everything from relationship issues to appropriate media boundaries for my kids. She has told me more than once that she thinks our generation is suffering from information overload. Too many experts giving us too many opinions on too many topics. The older I get, the more I tend to agree with her. One hates to look a gift horse in the mouth, but when it comes to the horse of expert advice, sometimes it feels as though we are getting kicked in the rear end. My mother's generation of women seems to have a confidence that my peers and I lack, and I think, in part, this lack of confidence is related to the plethora of opinions we are bombarded with each day. But I could be wrong, I'm no expert after all.

As a generation, we face a daily blitzkrieg of books and blogs, articles and scientific studies. Rather than feeling empowered with the information and advice we are given, we are left shell-shocked, a modern day David-the-Shepherd-Boy, weighed down in the king's armor and unable to move. Whether it be in our relationships, in our parenting, or in our spiritual lives, the stench of fear rises up from us like steam rising from hot asphalt after a down-pour. I see it in the young women who come to me for advice regarding dating, career choices, and family planning issues, as they constantly need to define and affirm their relationships and vocations. I see it in my circle of friends as we struggle to do right by our husbands, children, and communities. I see it in my own heart as I endeavor to love the Lord my God with all my heart and with all my soul and with all my strength (Deut. 6:5). We have become so saturated in the psychology of our culture and the warring opinions of the day, we don't know where to step, for fear of tumbling into failure.

As we struggle to maintain our identity in Christ, an identity based on the truths of the gospel, where do all these extra-biblical opinions fit in? How do we find our place in the body, that unique niche for which we have been specifically created while still being receptive to outside influences? So much of the information swirling around us seems to erode our sense of individuality rather than build it up. Is it possible to process helpful input without being drowned in the undertow? And what role do our mistakes in judgment and erroneous opinions play in shaping us for service? Where do we find the freedom to fail and live to fight another day?

Now I am not putting forth the theory that there is a grand conspiracy among all experts to paralyze us with fear and rob us of our sanity. Though this might make a good plot line for Steven Spielberg's next flick, I don't find this theory plausible off the big screen. The power of the experts comes not from conspiratorial mind control but from our willingness to give credence to their advice. They have the right to share their expertise, and it is then our responsibility to sift out the sanity-preserving information from the insanity-causing junk. While *Becoming a Woman of Excellence* is not included in the biblical canon and not every word from the mouth of James Dobson is inspired by the Holy Spirit, they still have some great things to teach us. We just need to figure out what those things are and ignore the rest. The "expert" voices in our heads aren't limited to the books and blogs we read or well-known personalities whose advise we respect. Our parents, friends, spouse, in-laws, and pastors all play an enormous role in shaping our opinions and ideas.

I first encountered the "experts" when Jim and I became engaged. Of course, people had given me advice before, but up until that point I had no real interest in listening to it. Suddenly, it seemed everywhere I turned someone was recommending a book on creating the perfect marriage or giving me their own perspective on how to achieve marital bliss. I am not the easiest person to give advice to, but I *wanted* to have the perfect marriage, so I eagerly accepted these recommendations and went to town reading them. Some of them were just plain bad and easy to ignore. Others, however, were more difficult to dismiss. They seemed to make good points but in the end left me feeling paranoid and insecure about whether or not I had what it takes to "succeed" as a wife.

One of the benefits of having a husband you highly respect is that he can talk you back from the ledge when it comes to the voices in your head. I would go to Jim convinced that we needed to be writing love letters to each

other every night and holding hands more or we were destined to be failures as husband and wife. He would listen,
tell me he loved me, and then go back to doing whatever it
was I had just interrupted. He knew that listening was often
all I needed and that I would eventually figure out that we
aren't the love-letter-writing-constant-hand-holding sort. In
the end, I realized that if I concentrated on being a faithful
follower of Jesus, the being a good wife thing would work
itself out in the end.

This was an important lesson that I have tried to apply to
all areas of my life. If I am struggling to understand how to
act in a particular relationship or situation, boiling it down
to the basic principle and then considering what the Bible
might have to say is the easiest way to solve the conundrum.
Most, if not all, of the expert advice out there boils down
to doing just that. Those giving the advice may have found
a creative or insightful way of doing the boiling, but in the
end it is the revelation we have been given that should be
our guide. When others give us counsel, we should always
weigh it against the truth of the Bible. For example, I might
hear a random piece of parenting advice on the radio one
day and suddenly decide that all my children are going to be
juvenile delinquents if we don't start implementing the prescribed method immediately. However, if I stop and think
for a minute, I might discover that we are already achieving
the end result, just using a different method that is more in
keeping with our family's personality.

We have also been given the insights of God within us
as we face decisions and difficulties. Jesus is the ultimate

in-house expert. He has knowledge of our hearts, knowing us better than we even know ourselves. But He also has knowledge of the end product, so to speak; He knows what lies ahead and what we will need to face it. Through prayer and Bible study, as we come to know Him better, the Holy Spirit is able to give us discernment and wisdom regarding ourselves as well. By only focusing on understanding ourselves better, we deny ourselves the necessary tools to do so. When we take the focus off ourselves and put it on Christ, God will grant us a more objective and accurate picture of ourselves as well as Himself. This God-centered way of thinking also puts our faults into perspective.

It might be that you are tempted to think too highly of yourself. If so, meditating on the Creator of the universe might make you reconsider the importance of that long jump record you set back in high school. If you lean in the other direction, constantly dwelling on your faults and limitations, being reminded of the fact that this Almighty and Holy God cares for and loves you might just be the ego boost you need. Either way, you can never go wrong turning your eyes to Jesus.

Too often we turn to human sources of wisdom because we want to be the ones that fix ourselves. We think if we study hard enough, we can think ourselves out of our sinfulness or protect ourselves from making mistakes along the way. The bad news is that there is no way to keep our lives from veering off in unexpected and scary ways. You can read every marriage book there is and still end up alone. You can read *Résumé Writing for Dummies* a hundred times and still end up unemployed. That's the bad news. The good news is that if we keep our eyes on the purpose of our lives, glorifying our heavenly Father, all roads lead to that end.

This isn't to say that we should ignore the resources available to us. There are times when this is entirely appropriate, if not essential. I personally love the fact that when faced with a particularly difficult question from the kids, say, how many inches are in a mile, I can go online for a visit with my friend Mr. Google and have the answer. When I want to find a new recipe or a fitting quote for a presentation I am doing, it is all there at my fingertips. But there is a dark side to all this finger-tapping and that is knowing where to draw the line. Ina Garten might have time to make individual centerpieces, cocktails, and rack of lamb for ten, but I just need to know how to make dinner for ten in under an hour and for less than $20. Queen Homeschool might have the ability to supervise fourteen children in their Latin and Advanced Mathematics lessons while making soap out of goat's milk, but I just need to come up with an activity to keep my kids busy while I get my blog post done. I do not want to put down women who seem to have boundless amounts of energy and pull off perfection without a hitch. They are out there and many are genuine and lovely ladies. But I also know that often we are presented with a very heavily edited version of these women's lives. These superwomen and all their cornucopias of knowledge should be a tool that makes our lives better, not a baseball bat with which we beat ourselves over the head.

Our wicked hearts often want to place these women atop a wobbly pedestal of our own expectations and then spitefully push them over. By recognizing we all occupy the same level plane, we have no need to elevate or tear down one another. If these women are believers, then they are aiming for the same goal and are on the same team. Our role might not be as high profile, but we are all working for God's glory. Our resentment probably says more about our desire to be glorified than it does about theirs.

Keeping the goal to glorify God with our lives, first and foremost in our minds, prevents us from unnecessarily eviscerating those around us and complaining about our role in the grand scheme. It also helps us to practice discernment when processing influences and advice. When you are reading a book, does it leave you feeling inspired and challenged to do more, to make better decisions, to up your God-service game? If so, read away and be thankful you stumbled upon this source of truth. If not, first start with your own heart and examine what is truly disturbing you. Is it your envy and insecurities? Or are the theories the book puts forth contrary to the wisdom and light we are given in Scripture?

Whether you bury yourself in the Bible or read the entire women's section of your local Christian bookstore, or both, you are going to mess up. You will not be the perfect girlfriend, or roommate, or wife, or mother. It is not a lack of knowledge that causes you and I to fall short in life, it is lack of godliness. The apostle Paul says, "I have the desire to do what is good, but I cannot carry it out. For what I do is not the good I want to do; no the evil I do not want to do—this I keep on doing" (Rom. 7:18–19). If Paul can't pull off perfection, I don't think I have a shot either. Just as too much information can wear down our sense of self, so too can our failures. I want to be this godly person but I keep failing, so does that mean that I really don't want to be godly?

According to Paul, it means I'm like him, which is certainly not an entirely bad thing. The gospel isn't good news to us only when we are dead in sin and condemned before God. The gospel is the good news that leans down to pick us up when we fall into sin again. The gospel is the good news that washes off the mud of our transgressions daily. When I fail, I am not disproving the truth of the good news, only confirming my need for a Savior. I must constantly remember why I want to succeed—because I am already saved. My success doesn't save me.

In the midst of all the craziness of writing my first book, I decided to take my kids camping. After all, there can never be too many stressful endeavors in one's life, right? Lots of it was awful and I will spare you the details. Let's just say that I was glad we hadn't brought any weapons, otherwise I might have had an armed mutiny on my hands. There were bright spots, however, and one of these was hiking. My kids have been hiking since they were old enough to be strapped to my chest and dragged along. For the most part, putting aside the occasional complaints over blisters and lack of sugary snacks to revive them, they do pretty well.

This hike was marked "rugged" on the map, and those park rangers were not kidding. After a steep descent, we hiked along a rock-strewn creek bed, surrounded by breathtaking bluffs and ancient trees. There was no real trail so we had to pick our way over the rocks while trying to avoid falling into the creek. It took some strategizing because sometimes the "path" was on one side of the water and sometimes it was on the other. I spent half my time looking down in order to avoid tripping and the other half looking ahead, trying to figure out the best way to get where I was trying to go. If I spent too much time looking down, I would find myself way off track. If I spent too much time looking up, I would find myself stumbling over an unseen obstacle or standing in knee-deep water. Interestingly, the kids didn't seem to struggle with this at all. They just hopped from rock to rock and enjoyed the journey without thinking too far ahead. Sometimes they waded into the water on purpose and then made their way back to dry land. Sometimes they stopped on the rocks and rested for a while before moving forward.

That night as I lay in the tent listening to the sounds of my children's snoring mixed with the hiss of my ever-deflating air mattress, it struck me how this effort to balance looking down and looking ahead is a lot like life. Looking down is analogous to how I live when I shut out all outside influences and commitments and focus on what is right in front of me. My kids, my husband, my own thoughts. Straightening the house, paying the bills, watching movies I have already seen a hundred times. I need this time in small doses, to keep my balance and not get over-whelmed with the vast possibilities which lie just outside my door and mind. But if I live this way for too long, it is easy for my thoughts to become "inbred." Without out-side opinions and interactions, my tunnel vision can often lead to a dead end. I find myself stranded and needing to backtrack. That's why it is important to "look up" and get my bearings. The advice of experts and friends (and friends who are experts) is an invaluable resource which enrich and challenge me in my various roles. Looking up helps me to remember where I am trying to go and what path is best to get me there. But look too far ahead or get too distracted from my surrounding and I end up stumbling and falling flat on my face. It is the balance of the two that lead me in the right directions.

When Solomon built the temple, all the materials were prepared off-site in order to preserve the peace of the temple mount. Only when the stones had been perfectly crafted were they carried to the site and put in place. We are God's stone, the raw material of His Holy Temple. Our journey through life is the chipping and sanding that prepare us for eternal service in His courts. He can use many tools in order to mold us according to His design. Sometimes it will be the truths given to us by the experts. But sometimes we will be shaped by the mistakes we make along the way. If we offer up our mistakes for redemption, these too can be part of the process of being made ready to enter His gates with thanksgiving in our hearts and His courts with praise.

Someday Jim and I would like to retrace our travels out West, only this time with the kids. The small two-person tent will be replaced with the eight-person foldable mini-house we have now. Homer's *Odyssey* will have to be replaced with Mary Pope Osborne's *Odyssey*, which has better pictures anyway. And our historical audio book will give way to *Frog and Toad Are Friends*. In other words, though the places will be the same, the trip will be very different. I would love to look up some of the people we visited, present our brood to them and say, "See, despite the piercing and the stupidity of youth, it's turned out okay so far. The tattoo is still there, like all the other mistakes and errors in judgment you can't see. But these marks have been redeemed by the stripes that heal." Surely He took up our pain and bore our suffering . . . "he was pierced for our transgressions, he was crushed for our iniquities; the punishment that brought us peace was on him, and by his wounds we are healed" (Isa. 53:4–5).

Jesus' perfection and the pain He endured for my sake is the cornerstone on which my salvation is built. My mistakes and transgressions are shaped into something beautiful by the Master Craftsman's hands. They are the stones paving my way to paradise, and I wouldn't trade a single one.

Chapter Eight

Wives and Girlfriends

*I won't say she was silly, but I think one
of us was silly, and it wasn't me!*
—Elizabeth Gaskell, *Wives and Daughters*

In a moment of bravery or stupidity, depending on your
perspective, I once rode one of those carnival rides that
demonstrates the principle of a centrifuge. The one my kids
thrill to ride every year is called the Gravitron. You stand
in a circular "room," which begins to spin faster and faster.
I am getting dizzy now just thinking about it. Eventually
the ride is going so fast that you are pressed against the wall
by the force of the spinning. That's when the floor drops

from underneath you, and you are suspended against the wall by nothing but a principle of physics. For some, this is thrilling. The kids scream with delight as they abandon themselves to the experience.

I scream right along with them, but my screams are not of delight but terror. For me, this experience does not inspire feelings of great joy but rather feelings of great nausea. I believe I threw up afterward and I am *certain* that I vowed to participate in no further explorations of centrifuges, or any other nausea-inducing principles of physics, in the future.

While I have faithfully kept this vow, sometimes I feel as though I live my life, especially as it relates to other people, inside that carnival ride, thrown against the wall by forces beyond my control, hoping that the principles holding me there will keep me from plummeting to the ground. It isn't so much that my relationships are completely out of control, but that they are out of *my* control. Though I want to throw my head back and laugh at the thrill of it all, I am more often hunched over the toilet, head forward, sick with fear. Fear of getting hurt, fear of disappointing, fear of rejection. Fear that if I get off the ride altogether, I will miss out on something really great. So I stay on and just hope I don't throw up all over my fellow riders.

All great dramas are based on some sort of tension. That's what makes them, well, dramatic. She loves him, but he doesn't know she exists. He loves her but her family doesn't approve. In fact, running throughout all of creation is a thread of tension. The drama in works of fiction reflects the tension we see around us every day. The lion wants to live and must eat, but the gazelle also wants to live and doesn't want to be eaten. We marvel at the beauty of nature and its capacity to produce all that we need, but we shudder at its power and potential to destroy as well as create. The entire created order seems held together in a centrifuge of competing forces.

As Christian women, you and I desire to be defined ultimately by our relationship with Jesus, but so much of our satisfaction (and dissatisfaction) with our lives comes from our earthly—rather than heavenly—relationships. There's nothing wrong with our pursuit of earthly relationships, of course. God has placed us together, in community, to serve and love one another, to enjoy one another's company. As God said in the garden, it is not good for us to be alone. But how do we maintain a healthy balance between investing and nurturing relationships—especially with our male counterparts—and still stay rooted in our identity as brides of Christ? We may have "come a long way, baby," but as women so much of our lives are defined by the men to whom we are committed. How can we honor that commitment, give ourselves over to it whole-heartedly and yet place the greatest value on our commitment to Christ?

All of this committing starts with dating. I must confess to holding a rather low opinion of modern Western dating practices. This opinion is based on my own experience as well as observations made from my perch as the wife of a university professor with a bird's-eye view of the college dating scene. To mix metaphors here, I think dating, as practiced by the youth of today, is for the birds. Jim and I are strongly committed to seeing our children through high school before they begin to date. I hope to see my kids experience life in high school and college, free from the emotional entanglements of dating. This is a topic we discuss with them often, laying down for them a foundational understanding of what our expectations are while they are living with us and what our hopes are for them once they move out.

For our kids, currently at ages twelve, nine, eight, and six, the opposite sex holds little appeal. The few on-screen, and usually animated, kisses they have seen are quickly labeled as "disgusting" or "the scariest part of the whole movie." Mom and Dad exchanging a peck on the cheek is cause for gagging noises and a quick exit. Here comes that tension again. For ultimately, way, way down the road, like so far down the road, you can't even see it from here, I want all my children to be happily married. I long for them to walk through life with a partner who is their foil, who complements their strengths and weaknesses, who will love them in sickness and health, etc. Jim and I pray for this and try to convince them that someday they might just change their minds and desire this as well. *Some*day. Definitely *not* today. And therein lies the mental tug of war between wanting them to experience the freedoms of youth and preaching the joys of commitment. What am I communicating about commitment if it is something to be put off, if it is something you experience after having fun? Marriage should be the meal they look forward to, but sometimes I fear I make it sound like overcooked brussels sprouts and a stale Twinkie.

I am usually pretty good about getting dinner on the table at a reasonable hour, but summertime always poses a challenge for me as swimming, baseball games, and bike rides give our otherwise structured life a run for its money. One night, dinner was really late and in order to prevent my children from eating one another, I let them eat the only thing that was ready—dessert. To make matters worse, the only reason it was ready was because it had been made by our good friend Little Debbie. The kids enjoyed the novelty of eating dessert first, but somehow it didn't hold the same thrill, perhaps because they hadn't "earned" it with their veggies and protein. Some of them didn't even finish and when the mac and cheese was finally ready, they dove into it like it was apple pie.

Married life can be the hearty meal that gives us nourishment and romance the sweet dessert that plays an important role in the meal. But if we indulge in too many sweets before we commit to sitting down at the table of marriage, it can lose its appeal. I want my kids to enjoy romance as a part of the entirety of marriage, when it has been earned with commitment and hard work.

Single life shouldn't be a diet of junk food, aiming only to please one's lower appetites. It should be a time of preparation, the veggies that earn our dessert. I was very unguarded in my pre-Jim life, and it has tainted the taste of my married life. Rather than nourishing my soul with a healthy portion of discipline and selflessness, I gorged myself on empty calories. Though I can't go back and undo those choices, for those of you who are currently on the road to matrimony, here are a few things I have picked up along the way that might make your journey a smoother one. These principles don't just apply to the journey, however. They can certainly be applied once you have reached your destination as well.

1. Guard your emotions as well as your body. A great deal of emphasis is placed on keeping oneself physically pure, as well it should be. But I have seen countless young women leave their hearts wide open only to have them trampled by young men who are either clueless or really mean. I know it's cool to hang out, talking into the wee hours, being "just friends"; but ladies, ladies—we just don't work that way. We bond through words. For the female mind, these late night chats are like verbal make-out sessions. Therefore we must be careful to play it safe until we know that his intentions are honorable. If you need a man to pour your heart out to, talk to Jesus. I hear He stays up really late and is a great listener. Psalm 10:7 tells us that the Lord hears "the desire of the afflicted" and encourages them and listens to their cries.

That isn't to say you can't have male friends, but they shouldn't be your best friends. Not only does this leave you vulnerable, if you get married these relationships will either grow more distant or be dangerous. Again, there is the tension between having well-rounded friendships and putting yourself at risk.

For those who are married, remembering how important communication is for us as women, we should set aside time to talk about what is on our minds, not just the events of the day or a recapping of *The Amazing Race* episode he missed. I have entrusted my heart to this man and therefore can verbally make out with him all I want, assuming that I give him a chance to talk as well.

2. If you have nothing in common with the person you are dating and his parents hate you and your friends hate him, this is not romantic; it's a bad idea. If you haven't seen how *Romeo and Juliet* ends (spoiler alert), they both die. The point of marriage is not to be tragically romantic but to reflect the love and commitment of Christ into the world. While dating involves lots of alone time and cuddling, marriage involves driving ten hours to spend Christmas with the in-laws and buying ever-bigger beds so you can both get a good night's sleep. Yes, it is important to have complementary strengths and weaknesses, and often your differences can act as the glue that attracts and holds you together. Ecclesiastes 4:12 says, "Though one may be overpowered, two can defend themselves. A cord of three strands is not quickly broken." As we weave ourselves together, our differences make us stronger. But when considering your prospective mate's weaknesses, be sure to magnify them by forty or fifty years and then decide whether or not his "laid-back disposition" or "protective mother" is really all that adorable. One of my favorite quotes from Dr. Laura Schlessinger is something along the lines of "Don't marry an orange and then expect it to turn into an apple." If you want an orange, great. If not, put him back in the proverbial fruit bowl for someone else to enjoy and move on.

If you have already made your choice out of the fruit bowl, remember this is the man you chose and that unless yours was an arranged marriage, no one forced this man on you. Sure, maybe you didn't know that he would leave his socks on the bedroom floor, but I bet he could never have guessed that you would use way too much toilet paper either. We all have faults so you might as well embrace his with the same grace you are looking for yourself.

3. Look at the opportunities and experiences that you have now not as a chance to sow your wild oats but rather as a chance to sow a harvest of righteousness. That doesn't mean you can't have fun. Sowing righteousness can be really fun. It just means that if, like me, you live your single life in selfishness, you will have a longer row to hoe in married life. Galatians 6:7 states, "Do not be deceived: God cannot be mocked. A man reaps what he sows." That which you sow in single life you and your spouse will reap in marriage. Travel, be an adventurer, take the dream job with long hours and bad pay. Just see these as stepping-stones in a journey toward a more mature you rather than a detour from the real you. On the other hand, don't hold back for fear of missing "the one." I don't believe there is only one person with whom you can truly be happy, but I do believe that God has given us clear directions as to how to be happily married. So fearlessly follow His calling, and it will lead you in the right direction.

If you have settled down with a mate, I hope that you had many great adventures before doing so. If you did, savor their memory but do not fall into nostalgia. Reliving "the good old days" can be fun, but it also becomes pornographic if it breeds discontentment for your present. If you didn't have those adventures, take heart. My sister and her husband embarked on an epic journey, moving halfway across the globe with four kids in tow. Maybe your biggest adventures still lie ahead.

In dating, as in life, grounding yourself in Christ is the best step you can take in the journey. Everyone's situation is going to be a little—or a lot—different. Our circumstances and our relationships are as diverse as we are, but the one constant is Jesus. I often make fun of a certain type of poorly written praise choruses by putting them in the "Jesus Is My Boyfriend" category, but in some ways this sentiment is right. He is the model of what we should hope for in our mates just as He is the model of what we should hope to be. If we remember that His commitment to us is so great that He was willing to lay down His life in order to secure our salvation, nothing will shake us in the end. Someday we will be with Him forever in that great dessert buffet in the sky.

Of course, the lessons don't end once you say, "I do." Just as the single and dating life is full of the pushing and pulling of conflicting desires, in marriage we can often act like a pair of powerful and stubborn magnets. Facing the right direction, we are drawn to one another and hold tight, but flip one magnet around and they will repel one another until they are placed back in harmony. This pushing and pulling within marriage was brought home to me one day when Jim and I were visiting friends at their nearby lake house. We spent a delightful day watching the kids swim and tube. Our friends, whom I'll call Mark and Kristin, asked if we, the hubby and I, wanted a turn tubing. I jumped at the chance and committed us both. After having spent years on the sidelines with the other breastfeeding, baby-growing, nap-supervising onlookers, I have enjoyed resuming my place in the "participants" category now that the kids have become more independent. Maybe this explains my disproportionate enthusiasm for clinging to a glorified life raft while being dragged around behind a fast-moving boat. I was giddy with freedom. It quickly became apparent, however, that my husband and I, while being compatible in more ways than I can count, have very different approaches when it comes to tubing. I was all for throwing caution to the wind, jumping the wake, and wildly swinging us from one side to the other. He was for digging in, sticking to the middle, and just hanging on. Despite our difference in technique, we had a great time, but I think each of us was a bit frustrated with the other, feeling as though we were working against one another rather than working together.

The contrasting styles of our personalities, which in large part help to make us work as a team, sometimes make it feel as though we are working toward different ends. The experience helped to clarify my thinking regarding certain aspects of marriage. Here are a few of the truisms I picked up along our bumpy ride:

1. Neither one of you is going to be entirely comfortable. Know this from the get-go and make the best of it. In marriage, as in tubing, you are two people occupying one space. Someone's elbow will occasionally be in the other's face. That's just the way the tube bounces. Don't look at the other person and assume that he has more freedoms or privileges than you. Don't accuse him of unjustly taking advantage of you. This usually results in his pointing out all the ways you unjustly take advantage of him. Unless you are being pushed off the raft altogether, give your spouse the benefit of the doubt, hold on and try to keep from knocking his teeth out. There are seasons in married life where one partner will have less to give and need more in return. But in most cases, the pendulum swings back to the middle eventually and then heads in your favor if you are just willing to ride it out.

This is something to keep in mind in any relationship, romantic or otherwise. As the saying goes, there are two sides to every story; and learning to see the other person's side, whether it be a husband, boyfriend, roommate, or sibling, will greatly increase your ability to be a peacemaker. Unless you are willing to exit the relationship altogether, there always needs to be some give and take from both sides.

2. Decide upon a generally agreed upon philosophy or approach before you are in motion. Once the momentum of marriage is going, there is little time for adjustment. Of course, you can shift places and do things on the fly, but this generally involves a great deal more effort once you are underway than it does before things get rolling. While Jim and I did not do this on the lake, we did do this early on in our relationship. Our guiding principles have evolved through the years, but we still refer back to them to make sure we are living up to our commitment to one another. These principles also serve as reminders of what we are trying to accomplish. Our modes of operation may be very different, but that doesn't mean we aren't headed in the same direction.

For instance, we agreed that if one person really likes something, be it an activity, food, book, or film, the other person was obligated to try it, once. We have similar tastes in most things, but there are definitely times when our tastes part company. I can't tell you the thrill of having Jim agree to read a book I really enjoyed or to try a bite of a new food off my plate. It's great if he likes it, but just him being willing to try makes me feel loved. I have noticed over the years, however, that I sometimes shut him out. In these instances I do not even give him a chance to try something because I am afraid he will make fun of my taste (which he has never done) or I refuse to read or talk about something that interests him because it takes more effort than I am willing to put forth. As the kids get older and I have more consecutive nights of sleep, I am trying to be more open.

This is a principle that can apply to any relationship. I will never forget the time my parents went to our favorite Indian restaurant on the outside chance that they would like it. They didn't but we really appreciated their willingness to try.

3. Remember whose driving the boat. The fact that I can lean hard and move us toward the wake or that Jim can drag his feet deep into the surf and keep us in the middle makes it feel like we are cocaptains, but in reality it is the person driving the boat who is in control. He can whip us around or keep things nice and easy, but in the end we are at His mercy and not each other's. I know I can trust Jim and I hope he feels the same way about me, but in the end I know that I don't have to cling to him for my ultimate safety. This is true of all of us as individuals as well as couples. This makes things a lot less scary in marriage and in life. With this thought in mind, in good times or in bad, in the smooth waters or in the rough, I can sit back and enjoy the ride.

As I struggle to hang out in this life-sized version of the Gravitron, I often curse the forces that hold me in place and highlight my helpless state. I want to be in harmony with those around me rather than always performing this dance of give and take in which someone always has to lose. The spiritual nausea that rises in my soul is a clear indication that something is not right. I want to write the drama in which everyone wins; where the lion gets to eat and the gazelle gets to live. But this sick feeling is one that I must learn to embrace because it is a sign that I am not home.

The part of my spirit that rebels against the pull of this planet longs to take flight, and yet I am held in place by a force greater than myself. Someday the Operator of this ride will give the "all clear" and say that it is safe for me to exit the ride. Someday the tension will all be washed away in a shower of angelic praises. Until then, I will stay put, knowing that when the floor gives way I won't be allowed to fall.

Chapter Nine

The Gracious Giant

"I have many beautiful flowers" he said; "but the children are the most beautiful flowers of all."
—Oscar Wilde, *The Selfish Giant*

Two women, four kids, a minivan full of snacks, travel games, and luggage—everything one needs to survive a long interstate trip. Everything, that is, except a full tank of gas. Actually, a mere half gallon of gas would have been celebrated, compared to the fumes that currently comprised the entirety of our fuel supply. Just as I realized that my friend Gwen and I had chatted our way through three hundred miles and $60 of petrol, the engine coughed and died.

Pulling onto the shoulder, I prayed while Gwen quickly called our husbands, who were driving just ahead of us, to explain the situation. We were coasting uphill and had little chance of making it to the top, let alone to the exit half a mile away. But somehow we crested that hill. Somehow the fumes in the tank gave us the momentum to keep going forward. The exit ramp was on a decline and we coasted a good quarter mile to the gas station and made it to the pumps. A divine mercy if ever I have seen one. The unsuspecting wedding guests at Cana could not have rejoiced more over their filled glasses than we did at our filled tank. Though we had neglected to seek out what we needed most, failing to refuel, despite having stopped for bathroom breaks, food breaks, and soda breaks (which then required more bathroom breaks), God spared us from a vacation disaster. Though we had been distracted by all the activity around us, He had provided us with the necessities. He transformed a potential tale of woe into one more story of His faithfulness.

One of the ridiculously difficult things about raising children is that they are constantly developing and changing so that just when you think you have them figured out, they throw you a curve, a new twist you never saw coming. They are like mutating viruses—as soon as you have become immune to their latest shenanigans, they develop a new strain to which you have yet to be exposed. While this constant shape-shifting is one of the greatest challenges of parenting, it is also one of the things that makes them so fascinating and wonderful. Just as you become accustomed to the adorable way they put their toes in their mouths, they start sitting up on their own. Maintaining an upright position old news? They start to crawl. Unfortunately, while children are capable of rapid development in ways that make their parents glow with pride, they are equally capable of developing skills that make their parents blush with shame. And sadly, despite having witnessed this transformation in countless instances of other people's children, rarely do you anticipate the change in your own. One minute they are angels from heaven, the next they more closely resemble something from a more subterranean realm.

You might not be able to identify with the parent side of this equation yet, but we all play the role of child opposite someone's role as parent in our lives. Unless you were raised by wolves, you have been the adapting, evolving wonder of someone's life. It may not have been a good experience for either party, but the parent-child relationship is part of the created order of things.

God, as the author of creation, has obviously established these relationships and we can learn a great deal from them. With that in mind, we can ponder how our relationship with our mortal parents reflects that with our heavenly One. As we consider our identities as daughters of heaven, how does this affect the way we see our parents as well as our perspective regarding our relationships with others?

How do we allow our relationship with divine perfection to fuel our imperfect relationships on earth?

We are told in Isaiah 55:9, "As the heavens are higher than the earth, so are my ways higher than your ways and my thoughts than your thoughts." Taking Him at His word, we have to assume He knows what He was up to, not only in the establishment of the parent and child dynamic as a whole, but also as He has placed each one of us with unique individuals we call Mom and Dad. In my case though, one might be tempted to question the fairness of God's judgment. My parents are model citizens both of this world and the next. I suppose if righteous Job can be stuck with financial disaster, the annihilation of his children, a nagging wife, and a really bad rash, then it is a sign of my parents' righteousness that they got stuck with me. I have always been a prickly one to handle, and they have suffered every scratch and bruise with seemingly endless patience. "Extremely willful" does not begin to describe my mule-like nature. A few years back, a woman from my home church shared with me that watching my godly parents suffer through my rebellious teen years was an encouragement to her in her own parenting, seeing that you can do everything right and still end up with a child who struggles. While I cringe at being the bad apple in this story, she had a point.

I wish I could blame external factors for my rebellious heart, but while I had some bumps in the road, I was loved and cared for by two great people, not to mention my loving and supporting extended family and friends. The key to understanding most of my poor choices is internal rather than external; it is nature rather than nurture. Theologically, of course, we can affirm the sinful heart of man but when you are confronted with the sinful habits of your own heart, it is far easier to run for the therapist's couch and blame your family gene pool for your troubles, rather than looking in the mirror. It is easier to point the finger at others and attempt to excuse the lack of harmony we often experience in our families. But if we want our familial relationships to be a light to those around us, as children, and as parents, we must grab hold of the truth with the tenacity of a toddler and refuse to let go.

The truth is that our hearts are broken, not in the my-boyfriend-just-broke-up-with-me-and–I'll-never-be-the-same kind of way, but in the separated-from-God-and-His–goodness-because-I'm-full-of-selfishness-and-deceit kind of way. Just as this affects our relationships with friends and spouses, our fallenness taints our relationships with our parents and children as well. While we might wish to escape into an alternate reality full of *Little House on the Prairie* Ma and Pa relationships, we must learn to see the frustration that arises from our closest relationships as a merciful gift. The disagreements and differences we have with our parents and our children are like a two-way mirror in which we can, on the one hand, gain insight into the hearts of those from whom we spring and, on the other, see our own reflection. In his first letter to the Corinthians, the apostle Paul says, "For now we see only a poor reflection as in a mirror; then we shall see face to face. Now I know in part; then I shall know fully, even as I am fully known" (13:12). The mirror might be cracked and dirty but it is a mirror nonetheless that we have been given in order to know ourselves and our Maker more clearly. While we may be tempted to look at our parents and see the source of all our problems, the closer we look, the more of ourselves and our own responsibility we will see.

When we think about our relationships with our parents, oftentimes the temptation is to gather up all of our bad habits and shortcomings, bundle them into a neat package of neglect or enablement, and dump it all on our parents' doorstep like so much dirty laundry. Are your parents responsible for messing you up in some way? Of course. No one is perfect and certainly some parents are less perfect than others, but it is your heavenly Father who is ultimately responsible for your care. If you want to have your imperfections laundered, then drop them off at His door, not to point fingers or make accusations but in order to seek what we so desperately need—the cleansing of our own sins as well as healing from the consequences of others' sinful behavior. Then and only then can we extend the grace we have been given to our grace-needing mothers and fathers.

When I graduated from college, my life took a moral nosedive and it scared me. I knew I had to do something to turn it around. So I went to a Christian counselor. After listening to my background and the laundry list of my bad habits, he proceeded to explain them away. A lack of communication with my parents, low self-esteem, and other typically drawn upon reasonings. At some point I began to tune him out when I realized that I was perfectly capable of self-diagnosis. There was nothing wrong with me psychologically; I was just behaving badly and needed to stop. I didn't need excuses; I needed a Savior. I needed grace.

Once I realized that I was in need of grace myself, not just forgiving grace but fixing grace, I began to understand that those around me, though they might be more mature and godly like my parents, were in need of the same grace. Grace isn't just forgiveness, it is forgiveness fueled by surrender. The forgiver surrenders their rights to justice and the forgiver acknowledges their inability to make the situation right. My parents had long since surrendered their lives in order to receive the grace that drove their actions. It was my turn to surrender not just my sins, but also my life in order to receive what I so desperately needed. With that grace in hand, that treasure beyond comparison, it was much easier to forgive the insignificant slights I had suffered at the hands of others.

Becoming a parent was another major step in helping me along in my journey toward gracious living. Understanding the complexities of parenthood from this side of the fence makes me marvel that my parents did as well as they did. As I attempt to make wise choices for my kids, my appreciation for my parents' wisdom grows. Maybe you didn't have wise parents. Maybe they weren't just unwise but actually cruel and abusive. If this is the case, then much of what I am saying here may not apply to your specific situation. However, I encourage you to lay your pain and brokenness at the foot of the cross of Christ and begin to move forward. In Him is the fellowship of our sufferings and only through

Him do we find true healing and restoration. If you are given the opportunity to be a mother yourself, then He is giving you a chance to redeem your parents' sins just as He has given me a chance to redeem my rebellion.

For those of you, like me, who had good parents who did the best they could, giving your parents the gift of grace should also encourage you to do the same for yourself. My dad is a big reader and can count on receiving at least one book when the holidays roll around. My sister Susan and I are guilty of choosing books we want to read just so we can borrow them once he has finished reading them. Forgiveness is like that. You give it to others because you want to have it as well. When you forgive your parents' poor choices, it makes it easier to forgive your own. Rather than viewing yourself as the monster from the black lagoon because you have lost your cool over spilled milk, you have more realistic expectations of yourself. You know you are trying your best and you know that God will be there to fill in the gaps.

One of Jesus' parables I find most uncomfortable to listen to is the story of the unmerciful servant (Matt. 18:21–35). Just when I am ready to shake my head in disgust at the first servant's obvious lack of gratitude after being forgiven much and then failing to forgive another servant little, I realize I am that servant. Our most intimate relationships often reveal the blackest corners of our hearts. I complain to my children about their complaining; I feel slighted when a friend forgets to ask about an event important to me, all the while neglecting to inquire about what is going on in her life. When I fail to forgive as I have been forgiven. When I don't obey the way

I ask to be obeyed. Though it humbles me greatly, it sends me running to the cross. Where else can I go? Seeing my shame, nailing my Brother to the cross, I know how much I have been forgiven. At the foot of the cross, I am transformed from the unmerciful servant into the thief by Jesus' side who turned to Him in repentance and faith at the very last moment possible. Undeserving of mercy but destined to be with Him in Paradise.

The cross serves not only as a reminder of God's love and mercy, that He would send His Son to die in our place, but also as a reminder of the fate of God's children here on earth. As Paul says, "If God is for us, who can be against us? He who did not spare his own Son, but gave him up for us all—how will he not also, along with him, graciously give us all things?" (Rom. 8:31–32). This might seem like one of those feel-good verses in which we get to wallow in the excess of God's love. Wallow away, but just remember that if God didn't spare His own Son, His perfect and blameless Son, then why would He spare his adopted children the pains and sufferings of this world? If we want to be joint heirs with Jesus, picking up the cross is part of the deal. This same passage in Romans 8 goes on to list some of the things that can't separate us from the love of God, including some of the really unpleasant things that Paul assumes we will face—distress, persecution, and danger among them. I say this not to scare you but rather to encourage in the face of the inevitable, which you have already faced and will face again. Suffering isn't a sign you aren't loved but rather a sign that you are a child of God.

Facing this suffering as a child of God is hard enough, but facing it in the lives of your children can seem unbearable. While Jim and I have yet to face real tragedy in the lives of our children, we have had enough near-misses that we can begin to imagine. Our son Sam in particular seems to have a knack for the traumatic, from broken or lost possessions to illnesses and household accidents. A few years back, Sam's face accidentally collided with Bailey's baseball bat. Seeing my boy's face covered in blood and hearing his cries of pain, I was desperate to comfort and helpless to heal. This wasn't the first or last time my child's pain will caused my heart to ache. But as a parent, I can look to our heavenly Father's example and see that my child's pain can bring redemption to the world. Not on the scale that Jesus' death did, of course. But little by little, tear by tear, all of it can work for His glory. As a child, I can trust in His faithfulness to bring joy from sorrow.

Sam's injury was the result of an accident, but of course sometimes the pain we suffer as well as the pain our children suffer isn't accidental. You can tell them not to jump on the bed, but the little monkeys who don't listen will fall off and bump their heads. Just as my parents couldn't force me to heed their warnings, neither can I truly impose my will on my children. My parents came to the conclusion that while you can do your best to guide and teach your children what is right, you are not ultimately responsible for their behavior and the same is true for my kids. I can't make them obey but what I can do is follow my parents' example and pray, pray, pray.

I say pray, but I don't mean just for the children in your life. That, of course, is an essential part of our fulfilling the Great Commission and investing in the children we hold near and dear. But what is just as essential is that you pray for yourself. The beast of sin and rebellion dwells within the heart of my child, but the same is true of me. When my bundles of joy start to feel more like burdens of sorrow, I can feel as if I too am being transformed into a creature I would rather not face in the mirror.

As a stay-at-home mom, I have sacrificed a great deal in order to parent my children, day in and day out. Okay, a great deal might be a stretch. It wasn't as if I was a high-powered attorney pulling in big bucks. I didn't trade high heels for the scruffy house slippers my children love to belittle, or eighteen-dollar salads for cheese ravioli at Fazoli's. Still there are days when I look at the pimply faced cashier at the local fast-food chain and am tempted to jump across the counter and beg her to trade places. Mommying is a long-term investment with few (however rewarding) short-term gains. When my children fail to appreciate the sacrifices I have made, it doesn't sit too well. And when they add insult to injury by throwing in a dose of public humiliation into the mix, I am tempted to reexamine the fine print of my job description.

This is when I have to remind myself that it isn't really my kids that I am making all these sacrifices for. They are not my Employer. They are merely the tools He uses to mold me into His finished product. Too often I treat my relationship with Him like a union negotiation rather than a covenant based on mercy. I feel entitled to certain wages for the hours I have put in. But this isn't *Let's Make a Deal*; this is about servanthood and death to self.

This bargaining is all about control. My children say, "If you buy us something from the dollar section of Target, we will give you forty-five minutes of stellar behavior." When they don't live up to their end of the bargain, sparks fly. As my children are getting older, I am learning to stop seeing them as chess pieces to be moved from this space to that space in predictable patterns. I can't control their reactions and emotions no matter how hard I try. I want to bribe them into being the people I want them to be, but I can't. I can only show them grace when they mess up and hope they will show it to me in kind.

I can't control the actions and plans of my heavenly Father anymore than I can control my kids. He is a gracious giant, towering over me in every sense of the word. Being a child of God isn't about striking a good bargain. This isn't the garage sale of grace. We have been at war with our Maker, and His terms of peace are complete surrender or nothing. For this surrender, we are granted amnesty and so much more. We are the prodigal son, coming home with our tail between our legs, ready to make a deal, and He is our Father, running to welcome us back into the fold. What have we left behind but a pig sty and starvation? What are we giving up but the appearance of control over our bankrupt life? Only my will and pride can hinder my enjoyment of His love.

On the road I travel, I have been given all I need and then some. I am well-supplied and heading in the right direction. But too often I fail to stop to refuel. I get distracted by all the activity around me and forget that I am running on grace, on borrowed fuel which must be replenished from its only source. I don't take advantage of that which has been provided for me and try to make it on my own. Though I profess to know my dependence, I act as if I can make it on my own. "I can squeeze another mile or two out of this tank. I can make it another day or two without praying, without having read my Bible, without confessing my utter need for Him." But eventually I run out of steam, sheer willpower counts for little and I am left stranded. Even then He is faithful to rescue, give me a lift and a refill. If only I will surrender.

Chapter Ten

The Well-Tamed Mind

The whole idea was odd and radical,
and we weren't sure it was even legal.
—Jessie Wise, coauthor of *The Well-Trained Mind*

Plowing through the aisles of Target, I try to move quickly and keep my head low. I am doing my best imitation of a cat burglar, cool and casual as if there is nothing amiss. From the looks I am getting, however, I am moving as covertly as a herd of stampeding buffalo.

From my behavior, you might think I am involved in some highly illegal behavior or perhaps just trying to avoid that extremely talkative person you always run into when you are in a hurry. But I have never shoplifted, unless you count the time I forgot about the can of Ovaltine I put in the baby's car seat. (Anyway, I went back and paid for that.) And *I* am the extremely talkative person you always run into when you are in a hurry, so it wasn't that either. I am simply trying to get through the store with a minimum amount of attention . . . and I'm failing miserably. I leave a trail of popcorn and spilled soda that would do Hansel and Gretel proud, not to mention the volume of my posse in comparison with those around us.

You see, it's the middle of the day in the middle of the week and most of the women in the store are pushing carts containing a small baby or toddler. They are quietly chatting with their children who are slobbering on their giant pretzels. I, on the other hand, am pushing a cart surrounded by four loud and oversized-looking children, all but one of whom are "school-aged."

I have committed the homeschooler's cardinal sin: leaving the house between the hours of 8:00 a.m. and 3:00 p.m. with all kids in tow. Were a school bus to pull up into the parking lot right now, I would be tempted to shove them all inside and walk away.

Nothing screams "Look at me! I'm countercultural!" like being spotted in Target at eleven in the morning with school-aged children. It's one thing to be countercultural in the privacy of your own home but quite another to make a public appearance. Like Daniel praying at the window, I am making my stand clear. I just hope there aren't any lions waiting for me in the Pet Care aisle.

I have always been a bit out of the mainstream when it comes to dress and ways of thinking. In high school my socks were often purposefully mismatched, I wore jewelry made from silverware, and founded the Ecology Club years before it was cool to go green. Back then, it felt cool to be different. Now, however, the ways in which I am different feel less like being a free spirit and more like being a stick in the mud. Being different feels old-fashioned rather than forward thinking. Still there are times when our faith calls us to look behind us for wisdom rather than look around us for approval.

Living in a culture that tolerates only tolerance, how do we espouse an absolute right and wrong and yet engage the world in a way that reflects the love of God? What are some areas where we are called to go against the flow rather than with it? And what do we do with those gray areas, where the call to be countercultural isn't heard by everyone or, if heard, is interpreted differently?

The Bible gives us good examples to follow when it comes to being countercultural. In the first chapter of Daniel, we are told that "Daniel resolved not to defile himself with the royal food and wine, and he asked the chief official for permission not to defile himself this way" (Dan. 1:8). Just imagine how popular this made Daniel with the guys. We, of course, see this as the first step in Daniel's long journey of courage. But at the time some of his friends were probably doing the Israelite version of eye-rolling. "What is Daniel trying to prove, anyway? We have lost our homeland. Why can't we just make the best of living in exile?" The difference between these two sets of people—Daniel and his fellow vegetarian teetotalers and those who capitulated to the ways of Babylon—was that the first group didn't *want* to feel at home among the pagans. They knew that being God's chosen people had nothing to do with geography and everything to do with their relationship to God and from that relationship flows their obedience. Notice, too, that Daniel's attitude didn't cause animosity between himself and the locals, as we are told that "God had caused the official to show favor and sympathy to Daniel" (Dan. 1:9). Daniel set himself apart not out of contempt for those around him or a desire to appear superior but rather out of a heart that looked heavenward for approval. Of course, later in his life, Daniel did experience persecution for his faithfulness to God. Nothing says "We don't appreciate your value system" like being thrown into a pit of hungry lions.

When we truly set our eyes on heaven, it will put us at odds with the culture around us, but if we do so in humility and faith we ultimately have nothing to fear. God may have mercy on us and choose to soften the hearts of our neighbors to the righteousness of our cause, as He did with Daniel. But then again, He may choose to test our resolve and purify us with the fire of persecution as He did Daniel's homeboys Shadrach, Meshach, and Abednego. These three showed the same kind of courage and in the face of death delivered one of my favorite lines of the Bible: "O Nebuchadnezzar, we do not need to defend ourselves before you in this matter. If we are thrown into the blazing furnace, the God we serve is able to save us from it, and he will rescue us from your hand, O king. But even if he does not, we want you to know, O king, that we will not serve your gods or worship the image of gold you have set up" (Dan. 3:16–18). They chose to obey no matter what the outcome, and we should follow their example. It may mean that we attract people to ourselves in some unexpected ways, or it may mean that no one wants to sit with us at lunch time but either way we are not really alone.

Jesus tells His disciples, "If the world hates you, keep in mind that it hated me first. If you belonged to the world, it would love you as its own. As it is, you do not belong to the world, but I have chosen you out of the world. That is why the world hates you" (John 15:18–19). So while we might long to get comfy and stay a while, we must follow what is right whether "the world" appreciates it or not. That isn't to say it's easy. Or that being chosen out of the world looks the same for everyone. If we all consider ourselves as missionaries, called to bring the gospel to those around us, then our lives will reflect the differences of the cultures to which we are called. Just as those who serve in China and Bolivia live very different lives, so those who live in rural America live very differently from those who live in the heart of New York City. While those of us ministering within our same primary culture are not missionaries in the strictest sense of the word, thematically the connections are definitely there—the point is to set aside the culture of this world and exchange it for the culture of Christ. Though the end product might be very different, the heart from which it flows should be the same.

I have tried to channel my countercultural ways into this river of truth. What a blessing it has been to see God take causes that I originally championed because no one else around me cared about them and re-craft them into areas I care for because I think it pleases Him. Like the dry bones of Ezekiel, God is putting flesh on my activism and bringing life to that which was dead and meaningless without Him. Though you may be called to different areas of concern, the principles which lie beneath each of our callings should be the same. The principles of stewardship, discipleship, and the importance of the mind are some of the fundamentals we should consider as we strive to be countercultural.

1. Stewardship of Creation: I mentioned the founding of the Ecology Club back in the day. Then it was mainly an excuse to be antiestablishment and put cool-looking Green Peace stickers on everything I owned. This concern for the environment was one of the reasons I was drawn to Taylor University. Among the Christian colleges I looked at, theirs was one of the few environmental studies programs available at the time. As the environmental movement has gained popularity, it has moved from fringe to center stage. I suppose, having all this love for "Mother Nature" crammed down my throat and that of my kids has lessened my affection for Mother Nature rather than increased it.

The accumulation of "Go Green" messages hurdled at my doorstep has begun to resemble a landfill of impressive proportions.

In the past Christians have used our dominion over the earth as an excuse for misusing resources (Gen. 1:26). But if we consider how we are ruled over by our Superior, how we are cared for and loved, how much more so should we "rule" with care? With regards to being caretakers of the planet, Christians should be leading the way. Our starting point might be different but our concern should be the same. When we talk about nature in our house, we start with God. After all, He's the one that made it. The secular discussion of this topic obviously excludes the Creator and so we end up with "Mother Nature" and "Maintenance Sprites." (This was an actual character in a highly over-politicized reader's theater the children and I once had the misfortune to witness a few years back.) For believers, discussions regarding topics such as recycling and reducing waste should be couched within the broader context of respect for God's creation and acting as responsible stewards for that with which we have been entrusted (Gen. 9:10; Ps. 36:6).

When it comes to environmental issues, being at odds with the surrounding culture can be hard. It is so prevalent in the nature and science-oriented programming, which can be otherwise so enjoyable and informative. There is also the baggage of historical wrongs done in the name of stewardship making it tricky for Christians to navigate this issue. But if we are rooted in the virtues of self-control and compassion for all God's creation, these virtues will naturally overflow into our daily habits and choices. These individual changes can make a huge impact on those around us as well as the health of our planet.

Of course, there are many ways to incorporate these principles in our lives, and no one is going to be able to practice all of them. One way we have done so is by becoming vegetarians. Jim isn't much of a crier and so when I heard him sobbing one night while doing research for an ethics class, I knew something big was afoot. He had been watching footage of factory farming practices, and from that point on we made a conscious effort to limit the amount of meat we consumed and then try and stick to free range. You will notice a few qualifiers in that statement. With four kids, a limited budget, and food allergies to take into consideration, it isn't always easy to live up to the ideals of a cruelty-free lifestyle. But we do our best and that's better than nothing. I still fear that when the teenage years hit we will find pepperoni pizza boxes, rather than drugs or alcohol, hidden under our kids beds. Wait a minute . . . I think I'm actually quite okay with that.

While you can limit your intake of meat and develop a greater awareness of just where meat comes from and the sacrifice it requires, there are also ways to develop a deeper connection with our veggies. Composting can greatly reduce our trash output. Good for the garden, good for the garbage man. It is amazing to see how God has woven lessons of truth into all of creation. Rotten banana peels and wilting lettuce leaves become nutrient-rich soil for other plants. Out of death comes new life. Composting also promotes lessons in virtue as he who empties the kitchen compost bin gets a lesson in self-denial for the greater good. We also have a small garden of basic veggies and have lobbied our Town Council to allow us to raise our own hens and are always looking for ways to connect with our food outside of the grocery story. One of my favorite memories was the year we made grape jelly as a family. We each had a hand in the process of picking, cleaning, and cooking the grapes. The kids couldn't have been more proud if they had produced jars filled with gold rather than jelly.

2. Sacrificial Discipleship: In shopping for free-range meat and other organic goodies, I have more than once gotten the "breeder stink eye" from cashiers and patrons. Those who value so much life on this planet don't always seem to regard children as a valuable part of the ecosystem. That could just be because my kids are loud and much more likely to break something than, say, a spotted owl. But I think they, and all their small-sized counterparts, are a great addition to our planet. I know they are already helping by teaching their mom a thing or two about self-sacrifice. Not everyone is cut out to have an above-average sized family and some of you aren't ready to have family at all or have ended that season in your life. But you can certainly invest in the lives of the children around you and help their parents guide them in the way they should go. We are called to make disciples, and research, as well as experience, has shown that the most effective way to do this is by raising children in the Christian faith.[1] There are no guarantees, but early exposure as well as years of being prayed and cared for by believers seems like a good start. It means so much to have college students, neighbors, and Sunday school teachers shaping my children's worldview in a positive way.

Jim and I see the children around us, not only our children, but our nieces and nephews, neighborhood kids, and Little League players, as a mission field. Other religions certainly take this responsibility seriously. Having a large family is not an excuse to neglect taking the gospel to full-grown people, but we also should not neglect the opportunities we have to impact the kingdom through our children and families.

Finally, while healthy families come in small as well as large packages, Jim and I have seen major fruit in the lives of our children as a direct result of being in a larger family. There are lessons of patience, tolerance, and self-sacrifice that arise in the day-to-day operations of our family that can be learned elsewhere, but require a bit more intentionality. We are learning these lessons along with them. Working alongside children in Vacation Bible School or mentoring programs through your local school is a great way to build up patience as well as shepherding little ones to Christ. Jesus tells us, "Let the little children come to me, and do not hinder them, for the kingdom of heaven belongs to such as these" (Matt. 19:14). But how can they know if we don't tell them?

3. Intentional Education: While I eagerly embraced our decisions in relation to stewardship and discipleship, even my desire to color outside of the lines has its limits, so when Jim started encouraging me to homeschool our kids, I balked. My only experience with homeschooling up to that point was a family I knew who were the poster family for "Why You Shouldn't Homeschool." But faced with the reality that we couldn't afford private school and feeling uneasy about sending our oldest to public elementary, I decided to give it a try. I felt confirmed in that decision after the first year, but we have continued to take it year by year, and child by child. After several years at home, our oldest two are now enrolled in a small Christian school and loving it. Maggie is being homeschooled, and Andrew is getting ready to head off to half-day kindergarten. The options for educating your children really are endless, and while that is a good thing, it can be overwhelming.

When making educational choices for your offspring, remember to take everything everyone tells you about their own experience with a grain of salt. Hannah Homeschool may describe the idyllic days she spends learning with her precious flock, and while I am not saying she is lying, she is either very fortunate or glossing over the gory details a bit. Like most rewarding enterprises in life, homeschooling is hard. Really, really hard. That doesn't mean you won't enjoy it in the grand scheme of things. Just don't expect everything to go right all the time simply because you are making a sacrificial choice. On the other hand, Polly Public School and Pam Private Education may not be entirely forthcoming about the pitfalls of their choices either. In the end, you have to decide what fits you best and go with it.

Having homeschooled now for five years, I can say there are a lot of benefits. I think my children are closer to one another and to me than we would otherwise be if they had gone away to school starting with kindergarten. Being closer involves rubbing one another the wrong way sometimes, but that is how God wears away our rough edges. There are negatives as well. There have been times when I was so worn out from teaching that I had little energy left for mommying. That is when I had to remind myself that my primary calling is to be my children's mother and for a season lay down my role as their teacher. It wasn't easy because for several years my identity had been wrapped up in being a homeschooler and I feared being judged a failure. But ultimately, we must value obedience over the opinions of others.

That's how our oldest two have ended up in private school, and I have seen its benefits as well. Being in school has allowed the boys to see other adults' perspectives and observe different styles of teaching. I can't speak personally to the public school experience, but we have friends who have made this choice work for them and we admire their desire to work redemptively from within the public system. There is a certain perspective that Christian kids going through public schools acquire that I appreciate. They seem less dogmatic than those who are schooled in an all Christian environment. While they hold strong to their own faith, they have had the experience of interacting with and enjoying the friendships of nonbelievers.

Whatever choice you make, wear it with pride but tread lightly on the decisions of those around you. As a homeschooler, I steer clear of homeschooling literature and blogs and would rather have run naked through the streets of Fairmount than attend a homeschooling convention, fearing the shattering of my ever-fragile mommy ego. I'm not sure this hermit-like existence is entirely healthy, but the alternative was to walk away from encounters with other moms feeling defeated rather than encouraged. Understand that your choices are just that and there is certainly a lot of gray out there. The important thing is to be a light wherever you are placed.

Education isn't just an issue for parents, however. You may not be weighing the options of private versus public, but education isn't a process that ends on the day you receive your diploma. Each day we all make choices that influence our thinking for better and for worse. I often hear Christians debate the moral merits of books, film, and music, but we must also train ourselves to consider the intellectual merits of these as well.

Whether you are pro and conning school choices for your children or sitcoms for yourself, remember that who you are is founded on the work of Christ on your behalf, not on what school your child attends or what is currently in your Netflix queue. Show grace to those around you just as you wish to be shown grace.

I think the intellectual choices we make should be like any other choice, reasoned out and prayed over in light of the gospel and our desire to live it out. It is part of the immense diversity of God's people and His plans for individuals lives that we can all take the same principles and apply them to very different situations and yet have the same goal in mind, to bring glory to Him and accomplish His work on earth.

I'm back in Target, feeling alone in a crowd, well, in two crowds actually. The crowd of children I call my own and the crowd of small children's mothers that seem to be avoiding eye contact. But then, above the pleas for another sip of my Diet Coke, I hear an all-too-familiar sound. It is the noise of another crowd, a crowd of should-be-in-school children. I look to see a familiar scene. One mom, four kids, and a big mess. We make eye contact and immediately I feel my spirit lift. I can't help but cry out, "We can do it, sister!" and she smiles an "Amen!" A trip to Target in the middle of the day might not be the most countercultural expression, but sometimes it's enough. Enough to let the world know we aren't ashamed. Enough to let our sisters know we are in this together.

Chapter Eleven

Our Devilish Friend

I have made up my mind that I must have money,
Pa. I feel that I can't beg it, borrow it, or steal it;
and so I have resolved that I must marry it.
—Charles Dickens, *Our Mutual Friend*

Alcoholics Anonymous will tell you that in order to conquer any addiction, you must take it one day at a time. Obviously they have never met an addiction the size of mine; otherwise they would amend that statement to "one hour at a time." Maybe the difference comes from the fact that it isn't alcohol (or heroin, crack, or any other such illegal substance) to which I am addicted. Until recently I was practically a slave to Diet Coke Polar Pops. Not just

Diet Coke and not just Polar Pops. No, something about the combination of that artificially sweetened bubbly goodness and that overly large Styrofoam cup made my heart go pitter-patter. Literally. I drank so much of the stuff it sent my heart into serious palpitations.

If you aren't privileged to be familiar with the Polar Pop, it is simply a very large, very cold fountain drink. I am sure you have some similar beverage at your local convenience store. I have now kicked the habit that held me prisoner for so many years, but it is a daily battle to stay clean. In the monotony of my daily life, the ritual of purchasing this little slice of aspartame heaven was something to look forward to, a reward for all my hard work. I'm not sure when the reward became a necessity, no longer something to look forward to but something deeply woven into the fabric of my life. It was this realization that inspired me to quit. The comfort I found had become an altar, no matter how small, at which I worshipped each day. While my near-obsession with the Polar Pop seemed harmless enough, there are days when I sucked down Diet Coke like a prayer to heaven, seeking comfort in the temporal and physical rather than the eternal and spiritual. And so with a heavy heart, I lay down my Styrofoam cup of gladness that I might look for God in less artificially flavored waters.

I am a great lover of ritual and look for patterns in everything in order to create new traditions and habits.

If we celebrate a particular holiday successfully (i.e., complaining is kept at a minimum and there are no trips to the emergency room), I decide we should celebrate that holiday the same way every year. If we visit a park or vacation spot and really enjoy ourselves (see the above mentioned conditions for what constitutes enjoyment), then I decide we should go there every year. (I also prefer to drink out of the same mug, eat the same breakfast every morning, and reread books again and again. It's a sickness, I know.)

All these things aren't necessarily bad. My love of tradition has resulted in fond memories of Mother's Day with lunch at Olive Garden followed by a bike ride and family camping trips to the beautiful Indiana Dunes. I feel affirmed in this love by the fact that God seems to like routine as well. Otherwise, why would He make the sun rise and fall each day in pretty much the same way and have the seasons follow one another in the same order? Universal truths and patterns are ever-present in His creation. If He likes order and routine, why shouldn't we who are created in His image? Perhaps the draw of routine is part of the *Imago Dei*.

But what happens when the routine is all we see? What happens when the physical ritual overshadows the spiritual reality? In our society we are bombarded with the temptations of the material, the seductive siren call of comfort and greed. How do we enjoy our lives as physical beings without ignoring the deeper truths of the invisible? Is there a way to avoid the pitfalls of materialism as we tread carefully down the path of life?

We travel a lot during the summer and holidays, and whenever a Sunday rolls around that we are out of town, our family makes a concerted effort to attend church wherever we happen to have landed. I say "our family" makes the effort, but in reality Jim and I make the effort toward church while our children make the effort toward sleeping in. We have had some good experiences of the body of Christ beyond our local congregation, some not so good and some downright comical.

Recently I decided I wanted to attend a Catholic church, having never been to Mass before. Jim and I had prepared the kids that the service was going to be very different from what they were used to. We had made it through almost the entire service without anyone from our pew shouting out "But *why* do I have to keep standing up, sitting down, and kneeling?" when a member of the congregation leaned in and told me he needed our two oldest kids to help with something. Rather than try to explain that we were Protestant, I gave Bailey and Sam a shove toward the aisle and threw them to the wolves. Confused and apprehensive, they fumbled through carrying the communion wine to the altar, looking all the while as though the wolves were going to gobble them up at any moment. They left unscathed but bewildered by the whole experience. Though the "routine" of the Mass had meaning for those who understood the symbolism behind it, for my kids it was just going through the motions. It was hard for them to see God behind all that standing up, kneeling, and sitting down.

I can live my life like that, filling it with so much activity that it's hard to see God's hand in it all. I say I am living for Him, but in the end I am just going through the motions and failing to remind myself for Whom all the motion is supposed to be. Though I wouldn't consider myself materialistic, if I tend to value the material over the immaterial I might need to rethink that assessment. If it quacks like a duck and walks like a duck, then it's probably a duck. If I talk like a materialist and shop like a materialist, then I am pretty sure I know what that makes me. It might be a matter of degrees, but does that really matter in the end? In a society where greed is not only accepted but openly encouraged, it is very easy for us as Christians to justify our love of material comforts through comparing ourselves to those around us and deciding we come out all right by comparison.

I remember hearing about a study that said once you make over $50,000 a year, increasing your income doesn't increase your satisfaction with life. I immediately began wondering *Do they mean gross or after taxes? Does it take into account family size?* Jesus said, "For where your treasure is, there your heart will be also" (Matt. 6:21). Jesus also said, "Not everyone who says to me, 'Lord, Lord,' will enter the kingdom of heaven, but only he who does the will of my Father who is in heaven. Many will say to me on that day, 'Lord, Lord, did we not prophesy in your name, and in your name drive out demons and perform many miracles?' Then I will tell them plainly, 'I never knew you. Away from me, you evildoers!'" (Matt. 7:21–23). Doing the Father's will certainly includes using wisely the resources He has entrusted to me.

One of the difficulties inherent in diagnosing materialism in our hearts is defining it. The words *materialism* or *consumerism* might bring to mind large houses filled with luxury furnishings and a jet-set lifestyle far beyond the reach of our income bracket. But while our checking account balance may not reach the sky, the god of materialism is more than willing to bend low and touch our more modest spending habits. When we allow our material comforts to crowd out our spiritual priorities, we are as guilty as the millionaire in the mansion.

Some of us desire not to spend money but to save it, squirreling away for the financial winters that may pop up now and again. Being fiscally responsible certainly isn't sinful; rather it is prudent and wise. But hoarding cash far beyond that which you need in order to create a safety net against disaster, relying on your monetary discipline rather than God's provision, is neither prudent nor wise. While we may use the resources God has given in order to provide for ourselves and those in our care, we must always be mindful that our ultimate security lies with God, not our savings.

Not all materialism takes the form of spending money. Love of comfort doesn't have to be displayed with cold, hard cash. It can be the hand that reaches for the snooze button rather than volunteering among the less fortunate, or finding time to make brownies and run to the store, but not to call a friend or write an encouraging e-mail. Our time is a great resource for good in this world, and it is something we have all been given. They say time is money and while my time is not billed by the hour, it is limited. How I "spend" it says a great deal about what I value most.

This may seem a bit harsh, but then God's commands often are. Consider Jesus' conversation with the man dubbed "The Rich Young Ruler." The guy came to Jesus and basically said, "Hey Jesus, what do I need to do in order to get into heaven?" Jesus gave him a list of dos and don'ts, at which point Mr. Rich Young Ruler must be feeling pretty good. He has done all those things. And then Jesus lowered the bomb. "If you want to be perfect, go, sell your possessions and give to the poor, and you will have treasure in heaven. Then come, follow me" (Matt. 19:21). Ouch. At this point I think I might be tempted to settle for less than perfection and I guess so was Mr. RYR. Matthew tells us that "When the young man heard this, he went away sad, because he had great wealth" (Matt. 19:22). Jesus then proceeded to point out just how tight the bonds of the material are when He told the disciples, "It is easier for a camel to go through the eye of a needle than for a rich man to enter the kingdom of God" (Matt. 19:24). Certainly not the most encouraging words for the would-be follower of Jesus, and certainly not for us when we consider that even the "poor" in our society tower over much of the world when it comes to living standards.

What might seem like cruelly high standards, however, do not reflect God's desire to suck the fun out of our lives but rather to inject a greater good into them. While we clamor for the cotton candy pleasures this world has to offer, He is all the while guiding us toward the apple pie a la mode, except this apple pie is not only delicious but good for you; it's kid-tested, Father-approved. And while it might be discouraging to reflect on the prerequisites of discipleship, we must remember that we are not applying under our name. We have been adopted into the family of God and given a new name. The requirements have been met by another. "With man this is impossible, but with God all things are possible" (Matt. 19:26).

So what does this mean for us? Are we called to sell everything we have and head out on some holy pilgrimage? I hope not, because I have some stuff that I really like and while I would be willing to sell off those pants that never fit right and the paintings Jim bought before we were married, I am highly attached to my Converse tennis shoes and my retro, but more than serviceable, double oven. I think it is okay for us to hang on to certain possessions as long as we keep their value in perspective and do not allow them to hinder our walk and put us at the risk of dismissing a higher calling.

While we may not be called to literally sell everything we own, we are still seeking after that which the Rich Young Ruler sought—salvation. If this is truly our goal, then we must be willing to give up anything in order to obtain it. It isn't the object itself that hinders, but rather our unwillingness to lay it down. Being married to an academic, I don't have many wealthy friends, but there are some among my acquaintances who wear their large income much more lightly than I wear my smaller income. They don't fritter away their money but rather see it for what it is, a tool to be used in service of others. I might not be capable of generosity on the scale that they are, but I am capable of giving to those in need and doing so in a self-sacrificial way.

Immediately after I graduated from college, I took a trip with InterVarsity to the Ukraine. I wish I could say I went out of a pure desire to share the gospel with the lost of the Ukraine, but this wouldn't be entirely accurate. Still spiritually lost myself, I went more because I knew and admired the leaders and my parents really wanted me to go, but God used this trip in a powerful way to show me the true meaning of generosity.

We each were assigned a roommate and lived at a "resort" on the Black Sea and, on the weekends, visited our roommates' families in the city. I was happy to buy my roommate a candy bar or soda on our trips into town. I was happy to do so because I had enough money to buy us each a candy bar. This was not the case with the Ukrainian students who would often purchase something to eat, give each person in the group a bite and end up with nothing to eat themselves. Generosity to the point of sacrifice is true generosity, and it was humbling to learn this lesson from those I came to teach about Jesus. We often refer to Jesus' sacrifice on our behalf. This certainly wasn't a half-hearted, I'll-Share-Because-I-Still-Have-So-Much-Left-Over kind of sacrifice. He died and gave His last breath for us; nothing held back.

This is one of the models of antimaterialism I try to practice, giving up something I might really want in order to be generous to someone else. I try to cheerfully offer the kids a bite of whatever I am eating (which works as a good dieting tool as well as a spiritual discipline). We sponsor an international child in need and, when things get tight, we downgrade a luxury rather than miss a payment for his necessities. I am not as good about sacrificing my time as I would like to be. I require time alone, to think and refuel, and too often find myself shooing the kids away so I can finish watching *Masterpiece Theater*. But I'm working on it. There is a balance there, whether it be in time or money, when you need to leave yourself enough of a reserve so that you don't give to the point of bankruptcy.

While Jesus gave His all for our sake, there is a sense in which He did have a reserve. During his lifetime He often took time away in order to replenish His spirit. I doubt He was kicking back watching *Pride and Prejudice,* but He withdrew when needed. On the cross He laid down His life in whole but knowing that it was His to pick up again. We, too, can lay down our resources and time—the entirety of our lives—without fear because we share not only in His sacrifice but in His resurrection. At the mouth of the tomb of her brother Lazarus, Jesus told our friend Martha, "I am the resurrection and the life. He who believes in me will live, even though he dies; and whoever lives by believing in me will never die." Do you believe this?" Her answer was, "Yes, Lord, I believe that you are the Christ, the Son of God, who was to come into the world" (John 11:25–27). We say we believe the same thing, but do our actions rise up and say otherwise?

If we believe that we are God's children, set apart and

saved, then why is it so hard for us to let go? Why do we stand at the tomb of this world, full of death and decay, and long to collect it as our own? I think it is the image of God in us but twisted and warped by our sinful flesh. The story of this world began with God calling the material into being. If we are truly His children, then this same desire to create—this same draw to the physical—is present in our spirits as well. We "create" ourselves through our appearance, our clothes and hairstyles; we design our homes through our choices in colors and decor. Everywhere we go, everywhere we are, we create a memory of our presence through the physical. God did this in the creation of the world, so that others might share in His glory, that He might make Himself known and worshipped. When we use the material to do the same, to cause others to praise Him and bring Him glory, then we are following in the footsteps of our Maker. But when we use the material in order to bring honor and glory to ourselves, to divert attention away from Him and onto ourselves, we are following in the footsteps of Satan.

In Matthew we are told of the temptation of Jesus in the desert. The first temptation Jesus faced was very much a physical one. Jesus, on the verge of beginning His earthly ministry and immediately following His baptism, went into the desert to fast and pray. After forty days we are told Satan came to tempt Him. The Bible, in a masterful understatement, tells us that Jesus was hungry. So the devil said, "Why don't You make Yourself a sandwich out of the stones. After all, You are the Son of God and certainly He would want

You to keep Your strength up." Sounds like a plan to me! But no, Jesus saw through Satan's scheme. He saw that what the devil was asking Him to do was to rely on something outside of God's plan in order to be satisfied. To prove His Sonship by outward signs. He replied, "Man shall not live on bread alone, but on every word that comes from the mouth of God" (Matt. 4:4), and went right on being hungry, though eventually God did send His angel to take care of Jesus—which I am sure included a really hearty snack!

In my own life all too often I don't detect our devilish friend's scheming in time and fall straight into the trap of deriving my value from the outward rather than the inward. I look at my appearance and possessions as marketing tools and sell my soul for the approval of others. I create a brand of self, a commodity of me, and when it is selling well, I feel loved and valued. And when it sits on the shelf, dusty and no longer fashionable, I feel rejected and unimportant. Or I value the outward signs of my faith, the rituals of church-going and verse-memorizing over the inward reality that these things do not make up who I am. They are empty traditions if not done in the knowledge of who God is and who He has made me to be. It's just a bunch of standing up, sitting down, and kneeling. Only when I bend the knee of my heart, only when I go to the altar with all that I have, only then do I find all that I need.

I mentioned that I have given up Diet Coke Polar Pop drinking, or at least greatly reduced my consumption. I still allow myself the occasional can of decaf. Being the addict that I am, I couldn't go cold turkey without replacing the habit with another so I traded it in for a love of flavored sparkling water. There is nothing artificial, just some bubbles and a squeeze of fruit flavoring. I endure some ridicule from my family who often take a sip only to quote Homer Simpson saying, "Hello? Flavor? Are you in there?" But it's enough for me. I have replaced my man-constructed artificiality with something more natural. These days I am filling my cup with only that which God has made and am always willing to share.

Chapter Twelve

The Mysterious Secular Society

The messages ride piggyback on signals.
Television, radio, cell phones—all these things
make use of invisible signals, and the Sender
has found a way to take advantage.
—Trenton Lee Stewart, *The Mysterious Benedict Society*

Standing with the door open and halfway into the van, I am swapping movie recommendations with our pastor as Jim and the kids wait patiently for me to finish yammering on and on about one of my favorite topics. Pastor Bob and his wife, Mary, share our love for film, and it is always a pleasure to exchange titles with them. Finally, the hungry, tired children can take no more. I get into the car and throw out one last title, qualifying my recommendation with the warning that the language is quite strong. "Unfortunately," I say, "there is a lot of the f-word." As I am settling into my seat, a sweet child's voice pipes up from the backseat, happy that he too can now participate in the conversation. "I know what the f-word is!" he proudly proclaims loudly, certainly loud enough that the shepherd of our flock is now aware that apparently our children have been exposed to excessively bad language. In shock, all heads swivel and stare, which is just the effect said child had hoped to create. I am holding my breath, wondering if I can make myself pass out in order to avoid any further humiliation. Giggling he declares, "It's *fart*!" Big exhale. Using my best you-got-me voice, I say "Yep, that's right. Fart." A quick good-bye to Pastor Bob and we are on our way. I lean back and remind myself this is what comes of staying after church too long. A narrow escape, but how long will it be until that innocent mind who can think of no dirtier word than "fart" will be faced with the foulness of our culture? How do I as a parent prepare him for the battle that lies ahead? And how do I prepare myself?

One of the first lessons I've learned as my children have grown older is that just as everyone has different approaches to potty training and bedtime routines and education, all families have different standards when it comes to pop culture. Some parents are more sensitive to violent content while others try harder to avoid inappropriate language; some shy away from sexual innuendo while others are more sensitive to the occult. These differing sensitivities aren't limited to families. As Christians, we all have different tolerances and guiding principles that determine what we will and won't watch. Pop culture, especially in the form of media such as film, television, books, and music, is everywhere, and as believers we are forced to engage in that culture whether we like it or not. The question is how to engage without compromising our moral standing.

With such widely differing opinions on what is and isn't appropriate for Christians to consume, how do we develop these guiding principles for ourselves? How should our understanding of the gospel and our position as adopted children of God inform our choices? For those of us who are parents, how do we protect our children from that which is bad in pop culture while teaching them to engage that which is good? And how do we hold one another accountable without being overly judgmental and without imposing our personal standards on others?

With six and half years between my oldest and youngest, every day I wrestle with how to accommodate four sets of sensitivities—five if you count my own. We don't receive television stations at all so our kids have to rely on DVDs from Netflix and the library along with the occasional visits to their grandparents' house for their intake of visual media. While this certainly simplifies a lot of things, it does make it tricky to choose something that everyone can, and wants, to watch. They each pick out their DVD of choice and then retreat to the trenches, ready to fight to the death over whether it's *Avatar, The Last Airbender,* or *Backyardigans.* Sometimes alliances form, generally along age groups but rarely do they all say in a unified and cheery voice "Yes, let's watch this one."

Breaking the stalemate then falls to me and I feel torn. I sympathize with the older ones who have said good-bye to *Dora the Explorer,* and frankly I was all too happy to watch her *vamanos* from the building. On the other hand, I feel for the younger ones and long to preserve their love for the more innocent, albeit sometimes irritating, content of such classics as *VeggieTales* and *Blue's Clues.* I think of Paul's admonition for the Romans who certainly knew a thing or two about living out your faith in an immoral and corrupt society. "Let us therefore make every effort to do what leads to peace and to mutual edification. Do not destroy the work of God for the sake of food. All food is clean, but it is wrong for a man to eat anything that causes someone else to stumble. It is better not to eat meat or drink wine or to do anything else that will cause your brother to fall" (Rom. 14:19–21). In their day and age, it was food that had been sacrificed to idols that was the issue, but we can easily apply this verse, inserting our own cultural struggles. For example, "Do not destroy the work of God for the sake of entertainment." Of course, not all entertainment is clean and there are obviously categories such as pornography, violent video games, and explicative-laden music, which can be easily dismissed as inappropriate for anyone. But that leaves a lot of gray area. Does Bailey not get to watch *Star Wars* because Andrew is too young to handle the more mature themes? Should I not purchase a song by P!nk for my workout playlist because she let's a potty-mouth word slip now and then?

This tension doesn't disappear as you get older. I remember once visiting a former student of Jim's and being sent to pick out a movie for us all to watch together. When I asked what type of content they avoided or were bothered by, the wife replied, "We take seriously the things that God takes seriously." Okay. I admire the principle, but what the heck does that mean?

Unfortunately for us, the Bible was written long before the invention of television, recorded music, and the Internet. Sadly, unlike the Ten Commandments, God did not hand Moses Ten Guidelines for Media Consumption for Children and Adults. Yet, despite the fact that Paul wasn't a member of Facebook and had no cell phone, there was certainly enough immorality in his own culture to give him reason to address it. As he closed his letter to the Philippians, he gave them a charge with which many of us are familiar, "Finally, brothers and sisters, whatever is true, whatever is noble, whatever is right, whatever is pure, whatever is lovely, whatever is admirable—if anything is excellent or praiseworthy—think about such things. Whatever you have learned or received or heard from me, or seen in me—put it into practice. And the God of peace will be with you" (Phil. 4:8–9). One could read this verse as another way of saying, "Take the things seriously that

God takes seriously." So what are those things? Things that are true, noble, right, pure, lovely, admirable, excellent, and praiseworthy.

It is doubtful that we will find anything outside of the Bible that is *all* of these things, but we can certainly train ourselves (and our children) to look for these qualities as well as their opposites. Just as we should be looking for these virtues, we should be on alert for their opposing vices. Several years ago Jim and I watched a film appropriately titled *Dangerous Beauty*. The movie was well-done from an aesthetic point of view but highly manipulative in its storytelling. So in the end as the "heroine" abandoned her virtue for the sake of her intellect, I found myself tempted to applaud her "courage." We have since used the phrase "dangerous beauty" to describe any film (or other artwork) that warps the truth in a clever or attractive way. They are beautiful on the outside but "on the inside are full of dead men's bones and everything unclean" (Matt. 23:27).

That isn't to say that everything I watch or let my children watch is free from false ideals or perspectives. Rather, I try to develop in myself and my kids an awareness of those falsehoods. We have talked to our children from an early age about looking for agendas within media. Someone has taken a great deal of time, trouble, and expense in order to produce this movie, book, or CD. So why are they doing so? To make money? Probably, but most often there is a secondary motive that has to do with the artist's view of the world. They may not want to go bankrupt but, as we say to the kids, everyone is trying to convince you of something.

I fear we have made our children paranoid when it comes to these messages lurking just beneath the surface of their favorite Nickelodeon show or hidden in the pages of their favorite novels. But as a wise person once said, just because you are paranoid, that doesn't mean they aren't out to get you.

When I stick with classics in literature and music—the more artistically inspired works that my children consider boring—I am in pretty safe territory. Art, by definition, reflects a certain thoughtfulness. Though I may disagree with the artist's interpretation of the truth, I go in expecting to really engage and wrestle with those interpretations. But there are plenty of nights when I am worn out, overwhelmed by all that was left undone, and the last thing I want to do is wrestle with Ingmar Bergman's perspective on the meaning of life. I want to drift into a world of easily resolved problems and predictably happy endings. There has to be a way in which I can indulge in a bit of escapism without risking my immortal soul. I definitely think there are ways to enjoy escape-hatch entertainment in small doses that don't threaten to sidetrack our spiritual growth. Everyone can eat a brownie now and again, but no one should eat them morning, noon, and night. And if I am living in a society where people are living off not just brownies, but brownies laced with poison, then I have to consider how my habits endorse or condemn the habits of others.

This is challenging because so much of our culture revolves around connecting through shared media experiences. "Did you see that show last night?" "Have you heard that new song by so and so?" No one wants to be the one saying, "No. I didn't catch that one because I find its objectification of women and promotion of homosexuality offensive." But if I don't say that, then who will? How can I complain about the content of television programming or the lack of quality reading material for children if I am unwilling to make a public stand against it?

This doesn't mean that you look for opportunities to preach the Gospel of Fluff Entertainment-Abstinence every chance you get. This will have little effect and probably only result in a significant decline in your popularity. But you can set an example for those around that preaches for you. And preach this gospel to yourself when making choices about what you will and won't watch. Consider Philippians 4:6–7, "Do not be anxious about anything, but in every situation, by prayer and petition, with thanksgiving, present your requests to God. And the peace of God, which transcends all understanding, will guard your hearts and your minds in Christ Jesus." We don't need to worry about how our choices might affect our hearts and minds. We need to *pray* about how they might be affected.

Of course, we can't just pray and then go about our entertainment business. The peace of God is not an invisible shield, protecting our souls despite whatever arrows we throw at it. Not only must we be active in the decision-making process, but we will be held accountable for the choices that we make. As our input of media influences our thinking, we will see the consequences of its influence. And adopted children or not, we will all one day stand before the throne and give an account of our time on this planet.

In light of the serious consequences of these choices, I have tried to develop principles by which to guide my decision making. I hope that sharing them with you will help in your quest to develop your own principles.

1. Throw away your television. Or at least, throw away your cable service. Before Jim and I were married, he made the decision to get rid of his TV. It wasn't an easy decision and stemmed not from his lack of interest in the programming but rather his overdeveloped interest in sports and news. This decision has been one of the most impactful decisions he could have made. Once Bailey was born and we could no longer run over to the university to watch a movie, we purchased a TV but only for video and eventually DVD use. We get plenty of TV time through our visits to friends and family. I am sure I would not be so sensitive to the foul language, nudity, and social agendas pouring into people's homes for hours each day if it were not for my limited exposure. I realize that TV is actually becoming an increasingly obsolete media source, and I now wrestle with how to avoid creating a quasi-television out of our computer and iPad. Sometimes I wrestle more effectively than others, but this decision has affected my marriage and family life in profound ways.

2. Consider approaching films, books, music, and more from an aesthetic perspective first and then a moral one. I know this might seem a bit backwards, but it works and can save you a lot of time and energy. Several years ago Christians got all worked up over the moral messages of *Titanic*. Seriously? Why bother? Granted the moral of the movie is that the key to a happy life is following your heart by sleeping with a guy you just met, abandoning your family to drown, and faking your own death. Nevertheless, it's just a bad movie. It's poorly written and acted. Why not just leave it at that?

In the same way, I scratch my head at people who will watch or read something simply because it is "Christian." I have read plenty of "Christian" works of fiction that promote the same romanticized, though less steamy, version of love as their secular counterparts. This idea is poison to the minds and hearts of women and yet it is rationalized as good because it doesn't have any sex or bad language in it. This happens to children as well who are subjected to mind-numbing drivel simply because it contains a moral message. I don't let my kids watch *SpongeBob* because I think it is a far cry from promoting intelligence, and I encourage them to watch *VeggieTales* because it not only promotes good morals but is extremely well done. There are, of course, many Christian works that reflect this value of excellence and moral quality. We shouldn't just give someone a free ride for being a bad writer because they are a brother or sister in the faith. Remember that one of the virtues Paul admonishes us to value is excellence.

3. Don't rely on secular sources to set your standards. Just as we shouldn't rely on the label of "Christian" to determine what we will and won't consume, we shouldn't rely on those in Hollywood or secular publishers and record labels and their criteria for evaluating material as the basis of our judgments regarding what is and isn't appropriate. Just because something is marketed for children doesn't mean it is age appropriate. I have seen many Happy Meal toys promoting entirely inappropriate movies and Disney Channel show stars be-bopping about in clothes I wouldn't want to see on a twenty-year-old. This is where we have to be discerning and never look for the easy way out.

4. Rather than sheltering yourself and your children from all pop culture, practice discernment with the media you do consume. And teach your children to do the same. Don't underestimate your children's ability to process the things they watch, read, and listen to. This doesn't mean you should have no boundaries but rather that while you act as their hedge against the world, you are simultaneously giving them the tools they need to build their own defenses. If my kids don't have the critical thinking skills to evaluate the themes and overarching ideas of culture, then how will they know the difference between good and bad? I do this with the shows they watch now in hopes that they will model it later in life. Praise what is deserving and tell them why it is worthy of praise. Don't just simply say, "We don't watch that because it's bad." Give them the reasons, when appropriate, why it deserves condemnation. We are in the process of widening the boundaries of what our older boys can watch and read, and it is scary. And it is sometimes awkward, such as when one of the boys excitedly tells a friend about something she is reading, and the friend informs him that book is bad and he shouldn't be reading it. But that is an opportunity for more conversation. I try to read along with them as much as I can, and though I sometimes long to return to my own reading level, I see the fruit we bear in those shared experiences and know that it will pay off in the end.

Sitting in a darkened theater one night, I vow to never, ever go blindly into a film with one of our kids again. Some friends with kids older than Bailey had invited us to the movies. We hadn't screened it beforehand and weren't far into the movie before realizing it was going to be a long two hours. The main character was a horse and he was the only positive character in the movie. All the human characters were evil but especially the military. I sat in horror and watched my two-year-old absorbing the idea that soldiers, who he was taught to honor and respect, were in fact bad. The movie was violent, dark, and cynical and couldn't end fast enough. Driving home, Bailey started asking questions about guns. Why did bad guys have guns? Why did good guys have guns? Jim answered that good guys had guns in order to protect us from bad guys with guns. Bailey unsatisfied by this logic asked, "But Daddy, why we need guns?" Thus began our son's introduction into critical thinking regarding pop culture. His journey, along with that of his brothers and sister, have included some shining moments and some colossal misjudgments. But it is a journey we are on together. A journey to redeem the world for God's glory, one word at a time.

Chapter Thirteen

Oh, the Places You'll Hide

You have brains in your head. You have feet in your shoes. You can steer yourself any direction you choose. You're on your own. And you know what you know. And YOU are the one who'll decide where to go.
—Dr. Seuss, *Oh, the Places You'll Go!*

Like a prisoner stumbling from the shadows of her dimly lit cell, I stand blinking in the fluorescent lights of freedom. I am stunned by my ability to move with such ease, unencumbered by my usual companions. I have managed to escape for a few minutes and feel overwhelmed by the possibilities. I am in the grocery store . . . alone! Near giddy with joy, I slowly wander the aisles, almost forgetting why I am here. I promised my cellmate, aka my husband, I would "just grab a few quick things and be right back." The car is running; the children are cranky, ready to eat and head for bed. But in the vast expanse before me, I lose focus and start thinking of all the supplies we need in addition to the essentials I came in to purchase. Somewhere in the baking supply aisle, a voice breaks through my blissful haze. Someone is calling my name, repeatedly directing me to meet my party at the front of the store. My party? I have arrived at my party and am enjoying it immensely, thank you very much. I cautiously turn my cart around, curious to see who I will meet. As I get closer, the sound of a wailing baby reaches my ears. Now I see my party. This party doesn't have balloons or streamers or drinks with decorative umbrellas in them. Just a weary husband holding a screaming and hungry baby, standing beside a cookie-besmudged toddler with an ear infection. Instantly I am transformed. Gone is the independent mover, the burden-free shopper on the go. While the scent of freedom still hangs in the air, I sigh and hold back the tears. As we walk out the door, my inner soundtrack begins to play. "It's my party and I'll cry if I want to . . . You would cry too if it happened to you."

There are days when my calling feels more like an episode of *ER* than *Full House*. It's more triage and four-sibling pile-ups than touching life lessons and adorable kids. I have always wanted to be doing what I am doing, but it's intense. Being a wife and mother sometimes feels like being an emergency physician who never gets to leave the hospital. Obviously there are breaks in the action, but you never know when someone is going to need immediate medical or emotional attention. Just as the calm lulls you into a feeling of false security, just as you log in to your favorite mind-numbing Web site or attempt to read a couple more pages of your novel, the alarm sounds and you are off and running. I once heard a female comedian describe a mother's free-time as being given a thousand dollars, only a nickel at a time. You know the breaks are there, but they are brief and unpredictable.

This is my experience of being a wife and mother, but moms certainly haven't cornered the market on busyness. Single women with demanding jobs and full social calendars. Young married women with major responsibilities in their communities and churches. Older women with grandkids and parents to look after. So much of how we define ourselves as individuals comes from what we do for others.

As caregivers of all sorts, how do we learn to care for ourselves? Whether you have children or not, all of us struggle with finding the balance between outwardly focused commitments and inwardly focused reflection. How many commitments does it take to make you overcommitted? On the other hand, when does investing in a little "me" time cross the line into the land of the narcissism?

One of my favorite resting activities is creating a sort of grown-up story hour for myself. Curling up in my favorite chair, wearing my comfy pants, and sipping from my "special" mug, I love to escape for an hour or two. I am a great lover of all things narrative. I love novels and movies, even not particularly good ones. I am happy to listen to a well-spun yarn shared by a friend over coffee and a snack. I will watch any PBS, History, or Discovery Health Channel show that has a good plot, whatever the subject matter.

I tend to approach the Bible from a narrative perspective, which isn't necessarily wrong. After all, it is a story— one grand story of God's redemptive plan and purpose. Obviously it is a story with a pretty famous author (God), but it is a story. I thrive on the characters; the intriguing twists and turns ("The walls fell down when they did what?"). Sometimes, however, I get a little too wrapped up in the characters. I start to take sides, play favorites. Peter vs. John? Totally Peter. How can you not love the guy who is getting a huge Jesus high five one minute and being called Satan the next? Elijah vs. Elisha? That one is a little bit trickier because I always get them confused, but I like the one who majorly taunts the pagan priests, calls down fire from heaven, and then runs away to the desert because he is afraid. If you haven't picked up on the not-so-subtle trend here, I tend to identify with the guys who come really close to getting it right and then fall flat on their faces. Like watching an infant taking his first steps, you really want to see them succeed but are holding your breath for the disastrous tumble you know is coming.

Of course, these stories haven't been given to us for their entertainment value but rather for our edification. We can learn much from the characters' examples, good and bad. As I said, I tend to gravitate toward the "bad" examples rather than the good. They shore up my ego a bit and serve to remind me that "God chose the foolish things of the world to shame the wise; God chose the weak things of the world to shame the strong. God chose the lowly things of this world and the despised things—and the things that are not—to nullify the things that are, so that no one may boast before him" (1 Cor. 1:27–29).

There aren't many women like this in the Bible. Most of those mentioned are of the never doubting, always believing sort. Ruth is loyal, Rahab shows great faith, and the Virgin Mary is humble in the face of great honor. Certainly these are women I strive to emulate, but despite my great respect for their faithful ways I just don't see us hanging out together. There are a few, though, that I definitely could see myself chatting on the phone with while my children run amuck and dinner burns on the stove: Sarah, a control freak who can't help but take things into her own hands and laughs at God's "alternative" plan; Rachel, who's frankly a big fat liar and a thief and a little whiny about the whole naming her kid "son of my trouble" thing (Gen. 35:18). These are women I can identify with—the ones that mess everything up and then complain about how messed up everything is.

In the New Testament there's Martha (Luke 10:38–42). Martha, Martha, Martha. How can you not love Martha, or at least feel really sorry for her? She is like the first-century version of Martha Stewart, wanting everything to be nice for her guests. And her guest is the Son of God, after all. Certainly if there is anyone for whom you want to make napkin animals, it would be Jesus, right? Isn't that what service is all about? Getting it right? I guess not, because despite the fact that she is working her tail off, probably whipping up a creative centerpiece and tasty hors d'oeuvres, Jesus doesn't seem too impressed. I can relate. While I wish to be Mary, listening at the feet of Jesus, doing the thing that is better, I know I would be the one running around like a chicken with its head cut off.

Martha is definitely in need of some balance in her life. It is obvious that she was well intended. After all, she opened her home to Jesus and the disciples. She was "worried and upset" for everything to go smoothly. I can just imagine her sticking her head out the kitchen door, wiping sweat from her brow, and what does she see but her little sister (you know Mary *has* to be the younger sister) just sitting on her duff. And to add insult to injury, when she appeals to Jesus for some justice, He takes Mary's side! Ouch. So where does Martha (and for that matter where do I) go wrong? After all, we are told to show our faith by our works (Phil. 2:12) and are given gifts and abilities in order that we might accomplish them. Too often, though, we are so busy exercising those gifts that we forget why we are running the race in the first place.

My exercise partner, Kristin, and I are always struggling to find times when we are both available in order to workout. Occasionally it will happen that we meet late one night only to meet early the next morning because it's the only time we both have free. Kristin's husband is always getting on to her about pushing herself too hard and not giving her muscles time to rest. We don't normally listen, but I always think of his advice when my shin splints start bothering me or my aching knees send a none-too-subtle signal that I have worked too hard. Our minds and spirits are the same way. They need rest in order to recover and refresh themselves. Otherwise, they ache with the strain of being pushed too hard.

But what does this resting look like? Does it mean we sit on the couch with a bag of Cheese Puffs and gorge ourselves on the artificiality of puffed "cheese" and romantic comedies? I fear not, or at least this is not the brand of renewal prescribed by Christ. If we look to the feet of Jesus, look to the place where Mary sat, that is where we find the rest that renews our minds and calms our spirits. That is where we find the rest from which we rise, ready to serve again.

And this should be the purpose of our resting. We shouldn't wield our quiet time like a sword, defending ourselves against the intrusions of others. I can't count the times I have growled at my children for interrupting my morning devotions. Of course, I need this time of reflection and renewal but when "I" and my "need" become the focus of this time, little good can come of it. Thinking of Mary at Jesus' feet, I doubt she was hanging out there in order to get out of doing the dishes or even out of a selfish desire to see what she could gain from being there. She was drawn to worship there and the benefits were an afterthought, a by-product of her adoration.

Unfortunately though for Mary, and for Martha, it is difficult to discern other people's motives from the outward appearance of things. Mary's "Yes" to Jesus looked to Martha like a "No" to helping with the "important work." This type of judgment regarding the motives of others certainly didn't end in the Mary/Martha living room. Any woman who has tried to secure enough nursery workers or volunteers for the school work day knows the gnawing doubts that can eat away at one's mind. We look at others who refuse to participate in our particular vocation or social activity and wonder if she really is too busy or if she just isn't interested. We can even have difficulty discerning our own motives. Being an introvert, I need time alone in order to function around others. But I can definitely use that as an excuse to keep from venturing outside my comfort zone. I can also use this time to focus on myself rather than turning my thoughts heavenward.

God, in His providence, has ensured that I have enough material for this book and has supplied many illustrations at the perfect time. Yesterday, I woke up exhausted from a long weekend trip with the kids, a sinus infection, and a dread of sitting down to work. While I would like to say that I made myself a strong cup of tea, took my antibiotic and prayed through the dread . . . that would be lying. Instead, I took my tea and my antibiotic, and retreated to bed where I proceeded to watch back-to-back episodes of a reality show too trivial to be named. Did this leave me rested and ready to face the day? Hardly. Later in the day I found myself frantically Swiffering my boys' room, crying and ranting about the Legos spilling over from every conceivable surface of their room. I may have "rested," but having approached this time with a sense of entitlement and selfish need, I did not rise from my bed renewed.

True, God-focused resting might feel like self-indulgent inactivity as well, but that is far from the truth as was once pointed out to me by my youngest child. Andrew is known for randomly producing exceedingly quotable lines from seemingly nowhere. Sometimes these gems deal with rather mundane topics as in the time he told us he couldn't help carry anything into the house because he was "full-handed" or the time he declared himself the "King of Potato Wedges." On other occasions, however, he perceives reality with a startling clarity that I suppose only the unpolluted vision of a child can produce. On one such occasion he turned to me with great certainty and confidence and said, "It's impossible to do nothing. Even if I am sitting here, I'm still doing something." While it might be tempting to relegate this statement to the "obvious bin," sometimes it is the obvious about which we most need to be reminded.

Even when I am sitting here, I am still doing something. Obviously this thought was lost on Martha who wanted to mark the occasion with busyness and frenzied preparation. It wasn't lost on Mary, though, who realized that sitting, waiting, listening is doing something. In fact, according to Jesus, it was the better thing. It was the only thing that was needed. Not the centerpieces or the napkin animals. Not the first-century cocktails or the sumptuous hors d'oeuvres.

Just sitting and listening. I am called to do the same. When I rest my spirit through the reading of God's Word and through prayer, I am not inactive at all. I am actively pursuing God's presence in my life, actively seeking the Holy Spirit and His work of redemption in my heart.

Sitting and listening sounds rather simple. Unfortunately, simple rarely means easy. It is simple to climb a mountain. Just put one foot in front of the other. But ask the climber, gasping for breath in the thin air of high elevation, if the climb is easy and I am sure her breathy response will be "Heck no!" The same is true for following in Mary's footsteps. Feeding first on the words of God is in many ways much more difficult than rushing around making fruit trays and hummus for Jesus and the boys. When I am physically active, I make an end product that is immediate and tangible. "Look at me. I just taught Sunday school. Put a star by my name and call me heaven bound." Of course, you can't see my heart. You can't know that in my heart I am grumbling that I had to get up twenty minutes earlier in order to be here. But when I wrestle with the Word and invite the Holy Spirit to search my heart, often I find things I would have rather left uncovered. Sitting still brings things to the surface I would rather leave submerged. But that same Word, which brings to light my weakness, promises to bring strength. "The LORD . . . gives strength to the weary and increases the power of the weak. Even youths grow tired and weary, and young men stumble and fall; but those who hope in the LORD will renew their strength. They will soar on wings like eagles; they will run and not grow weary, they will walk and not be faint" (Isa. 40:28–31).

Reading the Bible and praying aren't the only ways we can seek God and the power His presence and blessing bring. The truth is like a spring of water bubbling from God and flowing in many directions. It can be found in the laughter of a friend, the witty turn of a phrase by your favorite author, a touching scene in a well-made movie. We all need to drink from this fountain, but while the water is the same, our ways of collecting it differ. A big part of maturing is coming to understand what activities or disciplines you personally find refreshing. I have friends who come back from a weekend with friends beaming with energy, having been refreshed and encouraged. I am more of a one-on-one girl and enjoy spending time doing physical activities like hiking or riding bikes. That doesn't mean I don't need to spend time with my friends. It just means that time isn't how I rest but rather one of the things for which I rest up.

Whatever your method of recharging, it is crucial that you do so. It's not always easy to step back from responsibilities, whatever they may be, and carve out some time for yourself. For me, doing so requires depending on others to step in the gap I leave behind, which I find highly uncomfortable. I like to be the woman who can do it all, but when I act independently—refusing help from my Savior and my support staff of family and friends—I may be able to do it all but it is most likely all poorly done. Going away for a few hours or days isn't hiding from my responsibilities, it's preparing for them.

Just as we go to sleep with the idea that in the morning we will get up and face a new day of work, all this resting is, of course, the sleep that precedes the work. We are called to "lie down in green pastures" and refresh our souls because the darkest valley is just around the bend (Ps. 23:2). We learn to trust the Shepherd beside the still waters so that when faced with our enemies, it is to Him we turn for comfort. There seems to be a direct relationship between the amount of time one spends preparing and the number of difficulties one faces. We might think that the closer we draw to God, the less hardship we will encounter. But that would be wrong. If we use drawing close like an insurance policy against disaster, we are missing the point. It is more like a security blanket that we cling to in times of trouble. Charles Spurgeon says it best when he describes those who are looking for ease and those who are looking for God,

> He whose life is one even and smooth path will see but little of the glory of the Lord, for he has few occasions of self-emptying, and hence, but little fitness for being filled with the revelation of God . . . but they who "do business in great waters," these see his "wonders in the deep." Among the huge Atlantic-waves of bereavement, poverty, temptation, and reproach, we learn the power of Jehovah, because we feel the littleness of man . . . your trials have been the cleft of the rock in which Jehovah has set you, as

he did his servant Moses, that you might behold his glory as it passed by.[1]

So prepare your ship, sister. Gather your supplies and let us head for deep waters. We might face great storms, but we know where to hide when trouble comes.

My "party" is heading home—baby drifting off, *VeggieTales* blaring, toddler chattering away. I lean my head back and remember the quiet of those brief moments of freedom. But I must remind myself this isn't really prison. My cell is like that of Paul and Silas in Philippi; an earthquake has rocked my world, the doors are open, and the chains have been loosened (Acts 16). I am here to serve those around me. I have been called, not condemned. It is my party and I'll cry if I want to. But not tears of sadness or regret, rather tears of joy and gratitude. You would cry too if it happened to you.

Conclusion

The kids and I spend a great deal of our summer on the shores of Taylor Lake. While the "lake" would probably be classified a pond by experts, we don't mind. There is plenty of water for splashing each other, plenty of frogs and nonpoisonous snakes in the nearby woods for catching, and plenty of friends to share in both activities. One day this summer my writing had gone long, and we didn't arrive until late afternoon. The kids were disappointed that their friends were gone, but I was grateful for the peace and quiet. I settled into my chair on the beach and looked forward to reading my fluff book and drinking my oversized sparkling water.

About forty-five minutes later, I noticed a few families arriving, carrying covered dishes of salads and pasta and heading for the beachside pavilion. While moms carrying food is a common sight at the lake, dads are rare and the food is usually packaged in plastic and of the snack variety. A storm cloud gathered over my head and I suddenly realized it was Wednesday. On Wednesdays several families in the community bring dinner down to the beach and hang out together. It's an open invitation and by no means meant to be exclusive. Only I hadn't remembered the invitation and thus sat with neither a covered dish nor a husband in sight. I didn't think the fruit snacks and stale crackers I had would qualify as dinner, and Jim was committed elsewhere for the evening.

I quickly sent him a text for moral support. "I am being ambushed by happy families and pasta salad! Help!" Jim is sadly accustomed to receiving melodramatic and overstated communications from me and took it in stride. He then gave me some of the best advice ever. "Look for someone who needs a friend and talk with them. Stop thinking about yourself." While I was kind of hoping he would advise me to pack up quickly and retreat for home, I decided to give it a try. So I sat quietly and waited. Sure enough, a woman plopped down in the chair next to me and we chatted right up until the time her daughter threw up and she was needed elsewhere. I went back to sitting and soon someone else needed someone to hold her newborn while she chased after her toddler. I was happy to help. I kept looking around for ways to help rather than for ways to feel left out or slighted. The kids scraped out the remnants of a friend's brownies and seemed satisfied to wait for dinner if it meant they got to play with their friends. I even got a compliment from a young woman whose style I greatly admire. Victory snatched from the jaws of defeat, all because I listened to my husband's reasoned advice rather than the devil on my shoulder whispering words to feed my sense of inferiority.

On the way home I gave myself a little pat on the back: *You've come a long way, girl. You aren't home yet. But you're on your way.* From the outside my life may not look that much different. But I am being given a new heart, little by little, piece by piece. According to His promise, I am being given "an undivided heart" (Ezek. 11:19). This new heart is a gift, not something of my own making. God has removed my "heart of stone" and in its place He is giving me "a heart of flesh." It's not a heart formed by the law, but when it is complete, it will delight in the law. It will follow God's decrees and beat only for Him.

Right now, though, I am in heart limbo, somewhere between stone and flesh. I am the child in the womb, being formed slowly and with design but not yet complete. The stone is being flaked off bit by bit to reveal the live one underneath.

Moses, God's faithful prophet, took the rod into his own hands and acted outside of his Master's instructions (Num. 20:1–13), and for this he was denied entrance into the promised land. I have always thought this a harsh punishment for a man who served so faithfully among, let's face it, a rather unpleasant and frustrating group of people. If I were him, I would have beat the Israelites with the rod and left the rock alone. Still, God tells Moses that it was his lack of faith that destined him to die in the desert. But the Lord said to Moses and Aaron, "Because you did not trust in me enough to honor me as holy in the sight of the Israelites, you will not bring this community into the land I give them" (Num. 20:12).

We, sisters, are called to honor God as holy in the sight of those among whom we live. Whether it be our neighbors, coworkers, families, or friends, we must trust God to provide the water we need to keep going. When we remember our identity in Christ, it changes the way we see these relationships because we no longer base our worth on the approval of others but the approval we have already received from our Father through the work of His Son. When we remember who we are, we can face trials and suffering with hope because the gospel has changed the way we evaluate our circumstances. And so on with every aspect of our lives. The Good News is not just something that we hear once, accept, and then forget about it. It should be the foundation of our lives, of every decision and action we take.

At the end of his life, God took Moses to the top of Mount Nebo and showed him the promised land (Deut. 34). But that wasn't the end of Moses' journey. For when he had breathed his last earthly breath and was buried by God Himself, he arose from death into greater life in the promised land of heaven. This wasn't the promised land Moses was expecting to enter when he started his journey, but one that was infinitely greater. In the same way, we are standing on the mountain, peering off into the distance at the perfection that is to come. We have not yet finished our journey but we are closer every day.

Here on earth, there is a shadow of heaven, an earthly promised land of inner peace and joy. We find it when we act in faith, when we speak to the rock rather than striking at it. We find it when we trust in the Father's power, in the

Son's resurrection, and the Spirit's leading. We can choose to forsake these gifts and strike out on our own, grasping at a self-made perfection that is really no perfection at all. Or, like Moses, we can stand on the mountain and lay down our life, acknowledge our failure, and let our Father take us home. Now, on this side of the Jordan, we are exiles in waiting. But our destination is secure. We are arriving and yet still on the journey. We are dying so that we might come home.

Book Recommendations

The quotes I have used for the beginning of each chapter, as well as the slightly altered chapter titles, come from books that I hold near and dear to my heart. I love introducing people to my favorite works of fiction, almost as if I am acquainting one good friend with another. They are a mixture of books I have enjoyed personally and ones that I discovered or rediscovered with my kids. Here is a brief summary of each book and a few reasons why I think you will like them. I hope they will someday be your dear friends as well.

A Series of Unfortunate Events by **Lemony Snicket:** This is part of a series of cleverly written children's books that I look forward to my children reading. Though some might say it is a dark book due to the subject matter (three orphans pursued by a villain out to steal their fortune), it lacks cynicism, which I appreciate. The relationships between the siblings are touching, and there are lots of fun vocabulary lessons for children and adults as well.

***Vanity Fair* by William Makepeace Thackery:** I originally became acquainted with this novel through the film adaptation starring Reese Witherspoon. I was curious to see if the book was as sympathetic to the main character, Becky, but seeing as the subtitle is *A Novel Without a Hero,* you can guess the answer to that question. A difficult read because there are so many, well, vain people in it but a cautionary tale which certainly applies to our age as well as Thackery's.

***Crime and Punishment* by Fyodor Dostoevsky:** There are books I enjoy reading and books I enjoy having read. This one definitely falls into the latter category. Yes, it's long and at times difficult to understand. And yes, Russian people do strange things with their names that make it hard to follow at times, but this classic is worth the trouble. It centers around Rodion Romanovich Raskolnikov and his attempted justification of murder. It is filled with truth regarding sin and its consequences. Just don't try to read it when the kids are awake.

***Little House on the Prairie* by Laura Ingalls Wilder:** I grew up watching the television series and never knew what I was missing in the books. I love how Mrs. Wilder presents history in such a delightfully unconscious way. I have yet to convince any of my kids to read these independently, but they have enjoyed them as read-alouds, which gives me an excuse to read them as well. Provides great discussion on aspects of farm life which modern children have no concept of. Love the whole series!

***Great Expectations* by Charles Dickens:** This was the first Dickens book I ever read and there was no turning back after this. It's a bit heavier than most of his novels and the ending drives me nuts every time I think about it. Still, it's commentary on the effects of wealth on the soul are powerful. Dickens is a master of balancing weighty matters with humor as well as romance and love. I can't believe that all those characters lived in one person's head.

***Pride and Prejudice* by Jane Austen:** I can't remember if I read this or *Emma* first, but *P&P* is my second favorite Austen book and a must-read. I can't wait until my daughter Maggie is old enough to read it. You simply want the story to go on and on forever, thus all the modernizations of Austen's work. I half expect to find Elizabeth Bennett and her sisters in heaven along with Ms. Austen whom I plan to follow around and annoy for at least a million years.

***He Knew He Was Right* by Anthony Trollope:** A tragic story regarding the consequences of stubbornness and pride. A well-told though sad story of a young marriage that takes one wrong step with unforeseeable consequences. This is a very long book and rather depressing, so if you want to save yourself weeks of heartache, you could just watch the movie, which is very well done. It's just as sad, but at least it only lasts a few hours.

Wives and Daughters by Elizabeth Gaskell: I love all the works of Elizabeth Gaskell because she perfectly blends her Christian faith with a desire for social justice and wraps it up in a beautiful love story. I will warn you that Gaskell died before finishing this novel, so you have to imagine the last couple of chapters. There is a great BBC adaptation as well, which finishes the story for her. I recommend all of her novels especially *North and South,* which has nothing to do with the Civil War or Patrick Swayze.

The Selfish Giant by Oscar Wilde: I dare you to read this out loud and not cry at the end. Such a beautiful picture of grace and forgiveness. Our copy is wonderfully illustrated, and I enjoy the pictures almost as much as the words. A simple story of, as you might imagine, a selfish giant and his encounter with the gospel.

A Well-Trained Mind by Jessie Wise and Susan Wise Bauer: This is a homeschooling resource that has come in very handy to me but could be helpful even if you are just looking for a way to supplement what your kids are getting at school. Broken down by area of study and age, the book gives overviews of the literature available as well as great reading lists for children. There is also a version for adults, if you feel that your education was lacking in certain areas. Susan Wise Bauer has also written a history curriculum which I enjoyed, though my kids weren't totally sold on it.

***Our Mutual Friend* by Charles Dickens:** One of my favorite books of all time and definitely one of Dickens's best. It was also his last completed novel. The story of virtue amidst vice, love, overcoming obstacles of birth and rank. How does he manage to lecture us on the evils of greed, make us laugh at the folly of man, and cry at the beauty of love all in one book? Genius.

***The Mysterious Benedict Society* by Trenton Lee Stewart:** This was one I read along with our oldest and enjoyed as much as he did. Rich with social commentary, well written, suspenseful, funny, and touching. The story of three exceptionally gifted children who set out to foil the evil plans of the mysterious "Sender." One in a series and though I have only read the first book, I hear from Bailey they are all worth reading.

***Oh, the Places You Will Go* by Dr. Seuss:** No book list would be complete without at least one Dr. Seuss book and this is one of the best. I love his optimism and cleverness. This is one for the ages.

Letting Go of Perfect
This Week

So what now? You read this book, nodding your head in affirmation, saying to yourself *Yes! I need to let go of my expectations in my relationships and circumstances. I need to stop trying to be perfect and start being real. But I don't need help letting the dishes pile up in the sink or letting things slide. So how do I let go with purpose? How do I let go of my idea of perfect in order to grasp the perfection of God?*

Like the demons that shrieked and begged for mercy at the touch of Jesus, those habits of mind and body that hold us in bondage and prevent us from embracing the truth of the Good News die a slow and painful death. How do we prevent ourselves from making "letting go" just another thing to add to our to-do list? How do we not become perfectionistic about not being perfect?

Jesus battled those demons with the truth, the truth about who He was and what He was capable of doing. And so should we. So here are a few verses and possible applications to help you in your journey. Take a week to meditate on these Scriptures and ask God how you might apply them to your life. Allow the Word to speak freedom into your heart and mind just as Jesus did for those He touched. Remember, spending time in the Word and in prayer aren't items to go on your list; they aren't another burden to be carried through life. They are the list; they are life and through them you will be set free. Through them you will grasp perfection, all the while letting go.

Day One: Letting go of your busyness. This doesn't mean you get to lie on the couch all day and paint your toe nails. But it is important to rest in order to better serve. Just as our bodies need sleep, our minds and spirits need rest. Read Psalm 62:1–8. How can you find rest in God today? Try to put aside some non-essentials and just take time to enjoy the blessings God has given you.

Day Two: Letting go of your idols. You probably don't have an altar set up in your living room, but we all fashion "idols" out of things we don't think we can do without. Read 1 Corinthians 8:4–6. What idols are you relying on to give you satisfaction or security? Ask God to remove those idols from your heart and to remind you that He is the one true God.

Day Three: Letting go of your relationships. God has created us to be relational creatures. Our relationships with one another are important. But sometimes our perspective on those relationships becomes twisted. Read Ephesians 4:1–6. Ask God to grant you humility and patience in your relationships (just be prepared for Him to answer through embarrassing circumstances or annoying roommates). How might your relationships better reflect "a life worthy of the calling you have received"?

Day Four: Letting go of your expectations. We all have circumstances in our lives that don't meet up to our plans and expectations. But those circumstances are often the ones used by God to mold us according to His purpose. Read Hebrews 12:11–12. How can these verses alter your perspective on your current circumstances? Ask God to "strengthen your feeble arms and weak knees" so that you might accomplish the task He has given you.

Day Five: Letting go of your pride. They say pride comes before the fall but if by the "fall" we are referring to that whole apple eating incident in the garden of Eden, then pride came after. Read 1 Peter 5:6–7. Ask God to show you areas of your life where you need to humble yourself under His "mighty hand." Offer up your anxieties of being overlooked or under-valued to him so that He might "lift you up in due time."

Day Six: Letting go of your guilt. Just as pride can prevent us from acknowledging God's rightful lordship, guilt can prevent us from receiving His love. Read Galatians 5:1. Spend time thanking God for the freedom we have been offered in Christ. Confess the sins you have been carrying and leave the weight of their guilt behind you.

Day Seven: Grabbing hold of God's grace. The Christian life is a journey. While you have laid down these burdens and sins before God, I am sure, if you are anything like me, you will pick them, and others, up again and have to repeat the process. Read Ephesians 3:16–21. This is my prayer for you, just as it was Paul's prayer for the Ephesians. Each time you try to grab hold of perfection, ask God to loosen your grip so that you may "grasp how wide and long and high and deep is the love of Christ."

Notes

Chapter Four

1. *Chariots of Fire,* directed by Hugh Hudson, UK: Allied Stars Ltd. Presents An Enigma Production, 9 October 1981.

Chapter Ten

1. See http://www.barna.org/barna-update/article/5-barna-update/196-evangelism-is-most-effective-among-kids.

Chapter Thirteen

1. Charles Spurgeon, *Morning and Evening-Bible Gateway Devotionals,* July 19, 2011, (http://www.biblegateway.com/devotionals/morning-and-evening/2011/07/19).